Knowledge Management in Law Firms: Challenges and Opportunities Post-Pandemic

EDITED BY KATERINA MENHENNET

Commissioning editor
Katerina Menhennet

Managing director
Sian O'Neill

Knowledge Management in Law Firms: Challenges and Opportunities Post-Pandemic
is published by

Globe Law and Business Ltd
3 Mylor Close
Horsell
Woking
Surrey GU21 4DD
United Kingdom
Tel: +44 20 3745 4770
www.globelawandbusiness.com

Knowledge Management in Law Firms: Challenges and Opportunities Post-Pandemic

ISBN 9781787429437
EPUB ISBN 9781787429444
Adobe PDF ISBN 9781787429451

Contents

Executive summary ix

About the authors xvii

Chapter 1: Knowledge management strategies and frameworks for the post-COVID world
By Nick Milton, director and co-founder, Knoco Ltd
- Introduction 1
- The four main scenarios 1
- KM strategies for a new world 4
- How KM operated during lockdown and remote working 5
- A KM framework for a hybrid organization 8
- Conclusions 9

Chapter 2: Adapting legal knowledge management to the hybrid workplace
By Chris Boyd, chief operating officer, and Amy Halverson, director of knowledge management, research and information services, Wilson Sonsini Goodrich & Rosati
- Introduction 11
- The new legal workplace will be a hybrid one 11
- KM resources and practices will be key to making the hybrid workplace succeed 14
- Preparing KM for a hybrid future by cultivating connections 16
- Leveraging fully remote learnings to optimize KM for a hybrid world 17

Chapter 3: Social KM in a time of COVID… and beyond
By Ian Rodwell, head of client knowledge and learning, Linklaters LLP
The role of social KM 19
The impact of COVID-19 on social KM 21
"Rewilding" social KM in a COVID-emergent world 23
Concluding thoughts 25

Chapter 4: Knowledge management 2.0 – after the perfect storm, sailing with AI to new discoveries
By Joe Cohen, UKIME head of innovation, and Andrea Miskolczi, Europe director of innovation, Dentons
A perfect storm? 27
Keeping the good 28
Embracing the new 29
Beyond the old 31

Chapter 5: Data-driven knowledge-based management
By Jonna Vainikainen, business process manager, Castrén & Snellman Attorneys Ltd
The evolving role of knowledge management 33
Data quality – good enough and fit for purpose 34
Ensuring good-quality data – metrics and evaluation 36
The rising era of data-driven technologies and automatization 37
Legal industry trends call for good-quality data 40
Conclusion 42

Chapter 6: Legal technology and knowledge management
By Elisabeth Cappuyns, director of knowledge management, DLA Piper LLP (US)
Context 43
Developing trends 44
Overview of legal technology tools 45
Additional considerations 49
Conclusion 51

Chapter 7: Artificial intelligence and automation
By James Loft, COO, Rainbird Technologies
Artificial intelligence and automation in knowledge-driven industries 53
Unlocking automated decisioning 54
The combination of human potential and artificial intelligence 55
Technology ecosystems that support business growth 57

Chapter 8: Search
By Jon Beaumont, senior manager of knowledge management, Shearman & Sterling LLP
Introduction 61
Previously 61
Location and content 62
Basic approaches 63
Knowledge, data, and systems 65
Users and solutions 67
Results 69
The future 71

Chapter 9: Digital transformation, knowledge management, and cybersecurity in the post-COVID era
By Tiffany M. O'Neil, director of KM and technology innovation, and James G. Perkins, chief operating officer and chief compliance officer, Procopio, Cory, Hargreaves & Savitch LLP
Introduction 73
Digital mastery 74
Knowledge management and technology innovation 78
Cybersecurity 79
Protecting against attacks 80
Conclusion 84

Executive summary

Strategies for gathering and harnessing knowledge have existed in law firms for decades. However, knowledge management (KM) suddenly found itself in the spotlight as a result of the COVID-19 pandemic. Enforced remote working reduced opportunities for knowledge sharing between colleagues and this gap was filled with knowledge databases and experienced knowledge lawyers. Now that hybrid and virtual workforces are here to stay, these new working practices have combined with technological developments, enhanced demand, and the transformation of how to access knowledge to drive the advancement of knowledge management into a new era.

Knowledge Management in Law Firms: Challenges and Opportunities Post-Pandemic is the essential guide to the evolution of law firm knowledge management. In the chapters summarized below, an international group of KM experts share pandemic experiences and lessons learned, and provide guidance on how to prepare for and thrive in the knowledge management practices of the future.

Our opening chapter, written by Nick Milton, director and co-founder of Knoco Ltd, looks at the post-COVID landscape in two dimensions – firstly, what new activities and priorities an organization will face, and secondly, what new ways of working will be required. The former will set the strategy for KM, and the latter will address the nature of the KM framework itself and how this is affected by issues such as hybrid working. Remote and hybrid working provide many challenges to KM, including the strengthening of organizational silos and creation of additional barriers to cross-organizational knowledge sharing. Therefore, although the chapter acknowledges it is likely too early to say definitively what the post-COVID world will look like, if hybrid and remote working is here to stay, KM must become more intentional, and structures such as communities of practice will become as essential and deliberate a component of organizational life as teams and teamwork.

Taking the view that hybrid workforces are a permanent new

phenomenon, in our next chapter, Chris Boyd, chief operating officer, and Amy Halverson, director of knowledge management, research and information services at Wilson Sonsini Goodrich & Rosati, argue that the post-pandemic practice of law will leverage the benefits of both remote and in-office working. They explain how KM resources and practices supported the transition to remote work, including just-in-time content delivery, targeted communications, and virtual training, and how these will be key to making the hybrid workplace succeed. By showcasing some of the activities their firm has undertaken, the authors demonstrate how law firms can take advantage of the workflows and technologies that enabled remote work to foster knowledge-sharing practices in a hybrid environment that improve the way lawyers deliver value to clients, and create opportunities for training and engagement.

"Social KM" encompasses knowledge creation that emerges via the direct interaction of individuals (scheduled or unplanned), and is the focus of our third chapter. Ian Rodwell, head of client knowledge and learning at Linklaters LLP, studies the impact of the pandemic on social KM, and raises some of the key concerns and challenges that KM professionals and lawyers faced following the forced transition to remote working, and will likely continue to face as a hybrid working model is adopted. These include "information friction", reduced opportunities for osmotic learning, and the loss of serendipity. However, there are strategies law firms can use to "rewild" KM in a hybrid, post-COVID environment, several of which are outlined in this chapter, from protecting the liminal pause to facilitating osmosis. Ian concludes that the future of social KM still hangs in the balance, and it is therefore crucial that law firms utilize these strategies to stimulate connection and knowledge exchange.

With the advancement in recent years of machine learning, search, and NLP technologies, knowledge management teams have recognized the potential to utilize technology for harnessing know-how, and the power of data and data mining from legal documents, as a new superpower for law firms. A revolution around AI-assisted knowledge management started silently. Then the pandemic hit and knowledge management became front and center in law firms, with lawyers working from home increasingly relying on knowledge management teams and databases. Joe Cohen, UKIME head of innovation, and Andrea Miskolczi, Europe director of innovation at Dentons, believe that this has created the perfect storm and knowledge management 2.0 is on the horizon. In chapter four they explore the different types of assistance lawyers can increasingly expect from their AI-enhanced knowledge management systems, particularly in relation to knowledge submission and search, and demonstrate how combining new and relevant "old" practices can take knowledge management beyond its current limits.

Our next chapter tackles another important and growing talking point in the legal industry: data. In chapter five, Jonna Vainikainen, business process manager at Castrén & Snellman Attorneys Ltd, discusses the role of data in law firms and the transition from knowledge management to data-driven knowledge-based management that is currently ongoing in the legal sector. She begins by outlining the evolving role of knowledge management and the function's typical interactions with data to date, before focusing in on the topic of data quality. Jonna covers both why good-quality data is important, and how this good quality can be ensured, particularly through the use of appropriate metrics. Good-quality data plays a key role in the rise of data-driven technologies and automation, and a crucial part in many of the current legal industry trends, from the growing amount of data (and data sources varying in reliability) to sustainability. This chapter shows how knowledge management can help collect, assess, and harness this data.

Chapter six by Elisabeth Cappuyns, director of knowledge management at DLA Piper LLP (US), looks at the relationship between knowledge management and legal technology. She sets the scene with an explanation of the current context for legal technology and developing trends, such as the recent big investments in legal technology, changing client expectations, and the impact of the pandemic. Following this is an overview of some of the key recently developed legal technology tools and their KM applications, including communication and collaboration platforms, data analytics and data projects, matter profiling and experience management, and AI tools. Elisabeth also considers the adoption challenges relating to this legal tech, for example tech fatigue and increasing costs, and emphasizes the important role KM has to play in acquiring and implementing new technology, with the opportunity to identify and enact the best next steps to continue supporting the evolving practice of law.

Artificial intelligence and automation have for some time been considered too simplistic to handle the complexity and scale required for knowledge-intensive organizations. However, in chapter seven, James Loft, COO of Rainbird Technologies, explains why this is not the case and in fact there are many potential benefits of using artificial intelligence in the knowledge space. James discusses the rise of automated decision-making technology and how it can use codified expertise, data, and human interaction to arrive at the correct and most efficient outcomes. James' chapter also emphasizes how it is a combination of human potential and artificial intelligence that promises the most – for example codifying knowledge to turn personal expertise into organizational expertise – by understanding and accepting that humans and machines have different strengths and so should be trusted with different tasks. It concludes that any success with technology relies on an ecosystem approach, and that ecosystems of intelligent automation can work in alignment with specific organizational expectations to create tangible benefits for knowledge organizations.

Search is a key part of knowledge management, yet still to be truly mastered. In chapter eight, Jon Beaumont, senior manager of knowledge management at Shearman & Sterling LLP, firstly provides a brief history of knowledge in law firms and the rise in importance of search. This is followed by an analysis of the different aspects of search it is important to be aware of, such as the location and types of knowledge, including data; the current basic approaches to aiding search; expectations from lawyers; and considerations around data flow, integrations, and user experience. Jon also outlines the main requirements from lawyers when it comes to search, and provides guidance on how these can be met, such as through the use of filters and user data. The all-important issue of the presentation of search results is also addressed, covering both the positives and challenges, as well as the need to educate users on how to get the most out of their search experience. Finally, Jon ends with an optimistic look to the future, where continuing to embrace current developments will result in search becoming as valuable to lawyers as its potential promises.

Chapter nine takes a step back to provide a strategic overview of the use of technology in law firms, and focuses on digital transformation in the legal industry, knowledge management and technology innovation, and cybersecurity. Tiffany M. O'Neil, director of KM and technology innovation, and James G. Perkins, chief operating officer and chief compliance officer at Procopio, Cory, Hargreaves & Savitch LLP, discuss the path of digital transformation law firms are on, and provide a variety of lenses through which law firms can view their progress. They observe that, in order to move forward, law firms require technological innovation, and share how their firm has approached this with the formation of a Technology Innovation Group, which enables all of the new AI-enabled KM products. Finally, the authors highlight that behind every digital transformation lies the need to protect digital activities, knowledge, and data, and so they devote the latter sections of the chapter to the four-pronged method their firm uses to protect against attacks.

Turning our attention to the people involved in knowledge management, in recent years, many law firm knowledge management leaders have slid over into innovation roles, while often retaining their KM responsibilities. While this may at first be questioned, chapter ten by Gordon Vala-Webb, thought leader, speaker/author, and innovation professional, argues that the two disciplines have many similarities, and there is in fact a natural progression from KM to innovation roles. Both lean heavily – although not exclusively – on the use of new technologies; both require you to understand – at a very fundamental level – how your firm (or legal department) works; and both mean you need to be skilled at communicating complex and novel ideas to build willingness to make change. Gordon examines these three perspectives on the inter-connection between KM and innovation in detail, demonstrating that successful knowledge managers are well-placed to engage in innovation work. So, rather than KM and innovation being opposed concepts, they are actually twins, albeit with differences that make them more fraternal than identical. To conclude, Gordon offers some advice on how KM teams and leaders can begin their transition into the innovation realm.

Just as with other KM disciplines, competitive intelligence (CI) must be adapted for a hybrid workplace, and chapter 11 by Mark Gediman, senior research analyst at Alston & Bird, LLP, and Kevin Miles, manager, research services at Norton Rose Fulbright, guides us through the transitions for CI in and out of the pandemic. The authors explore the strengths and opportunities for CI presented by the culture shift, and how to manage expectations in a hybrid environment. They also share some commonly used virtual tools that greatly benefit CI professionals in a hybrid workplace, and demonstrate that some things are constant, for example ethics remains an important part of CI, especially so when research is being conducted remotely. Tables and examples are used to illustrate best CI practices in the future, hybrid workplace.

The talent war is raging across law firms and knowledge management is no exception. Our next chapter by Tara Pichardo-Angadi, head of knowledge (EMEA) at Norton Rose Fulbright LLP, provides guidance on how to manage your KM team and retain talent, taking into account three key areas as well as considerations post-COVID. The first of these areas is hiring, and Tara poses questions KM teams should ask themselves when recruiting talent. She also emphasizes the role of good onboarding. The second area is development, where the impact of team structure is discussed, as well as the importance of regular one-to-ones, helping KM talent build their network, creating a culture of open feedback, and training opportunities. The third and final area revolves around moving – Tara demonstrates why you must have regular career discussions and a clear career structure for KM, how you can foster a culture of loving what you do and doing what you love, and breaking down silos between teams. However, not all talent can stay permanently, and so the chapter concludes with advice on how to let team members go but create positive ambassadors for your firm's KM team.

A firm's approach to inclusion and diversity (I&D) is increasingly important to talent, and chapter 13 looks at I&D in knowledge, with a particular focus on best practice in the hybrid, post-COVID world. Orla Bingham, service owner, content development, and Katherine Lang, senior knowledge lawyer and London knowledge lead at Baker McKenzie, share some of their firm's key initiatives and learnings in relation to I&D. These include best practices in inclusive training, especially hybrid training sessions, embedding inclusive language throughout the firm, from knowledge repositories to day-to-day interactions, and how to ensure inclusion of all colleagues through mentoring programs. The authors also cover the importance of allyship in knowledge and how to encourage colleagues to be allies, normalizing the idea of bringing your whole self to work, and both the concerns and opportunities posed by the post-COVID return to work. The chapter is threaded with practical recommendations on embedding these best practices, and considers how I&D efforts can be continued going forward.

Our penultimate chapter by Kathy Skinner, director of research at White & Case LLP, analyses the impact of the pandemic on global research teams, and provides strategies for these teams to respond to some of the resulting challenges, and realize the opportunities created. Kathy observes that the transition to remote and hybrid working demands new ways to manage teams, and considers some of the biggest long-term challenges faced by global research teams, including those relating to talent, organizational structure, and team operations. Practical strategies and lists of top tips are included to provide a myriad of ideas on how to face these challenges and harness the potential benefits arising from the new way of working. As fraught and chaotic as the abrupt move to remote work was, it has created lasting change and transformative opportunities for research teams to embrace, including the potential to develop and provide new opportunities to team members, and to build more compelling and visible offerings to internal and external clients.

Advancing beyond hybrid and virtual working, the metaverse – a virtual space where people can work and socialize just as they do in real life – is becoming integrated into the consciousness of businesses and will create a whole new working environment. It will enhance the geographic reach of lawyers and law firms, enabling an increased access to knowledge, but there are important factors to consider to ensure this occurs successfully. The final chapter of this book, written by Anthony J. Rhem, CEO and principal consultant at AJ Rhem & Associates Inc., explores the metaverse and details how it will impact law firm KM. It covers metaverse drivers for law firm knowledge management, and how legal research, collaboration, ethics, and knowledge continuity will evolve in the metaverse. More and more clients are entering this space, and so Anthony concludes with some key pieces of advice for firms that wish to follow.

About the authors

Jon Beaumont is senior manager of knowledge management at Shearman & Sterling LLP. He is part of the global knowledge and research team that supports the organization's 24 offices. The team numbers approximately 40 individuals and sits under an 80-strong wider team consisting of legal project management and conflicts/new business intake (collectively known as the "client value team"). Jon oversees a global team of eight and is primarily responsible for document/matter management, search, translation services, document automation, and client collaboration. The team is involved in any knowledge-related projects, which vary hugely from analytics to data architecture to client consultancy. Previously with Shakespeares for 13 years, Jon progressed from information officer to head of knowledge management before departing for Shearman in 2014. Jon is a co-chair of the International Legal Technology Association (ILTA) knowledge management group, previous chair of the Recommind Decisiv Search Group, and a former BIALL council member.

Orla Bingham is a service owner for content development at Baker McKenzie, based in Belfast. Her role focuses on managing content development activities and services globally within knowledge and overseeing a team of paralegals and lawyers producing multijurisdictional guides and tools, client updates and alerts, trends, training materials, and development and automation of precedents. Orla joined the knowledge team at Baker McKenzie in 2018, and has previously held roles as a knowledge services manager, and knowledge lawyer for the Global Employment and Compensation group. She is a member of the Baker McKenzie Knowledge I&D Committee, supporting allyship and I&D initiatives across the function, as well as the Belfast Gender Committee, which promotes and creates group discussions around the significance of gender and broader I&D considerations in the firm. Prior to joining the Baker McKenzie knowledge function, Orla practiced as an employment solicitor in London, acting for commercial and private clients, undertaking both litigation and advisory work. Orla obtained her law degree from the University of Newcastle Upon Tyne, and her Legal Practice Certificate from the College of Law in Manchester.

Chris Boyd is the chief operating officer of Wilson Sonsini Goodrich & Rosati in Palo Alto, California. Chris leads the teams that handle attorney recruiting, business development, diversity and inclusion, human resources, knowledge management, marketing, practice management, professional development, research and information services, and work allocation. These teams work with firm, department, and practice group leaders to develop, deploy, and continuously improve processes, programs, and tools that support the firm's business goals and help the firm deliver more value to clients. Chris has an undergraduate degree from Princeton University and a law degree from Stanford Law School. He previously worked as a management consultant, corporate and securities attorney, and technology company knowledge management leader. He is a member of the board of directors of the International Legal Technology Association and is a fellow of the College of Law Practice Management.

Elisabeth Cappuyns is the director of knowledge management for DLA Piper LLP (US), a global law firm. In this role, she creates and implements knowledge management strategies and programs for attorneys and their groups to help optimize the practice and business of law, including by using technology and innovative solutions. Before shifting her focus to knowledge management in 2013, she practiced corporate law for over 15 years at law firms in New York, London, and Abu Dhabi, with a focus on M&A, private equity, and capital markets transactions. She holds a JD from Columbia Law School (New York) and a BA from Drew University (New Jersey), plus a Candidate in Law (in Dutch) from the University of Louvain (Belgium).

Joe Cohen is the head of innovation for Dentons' UK and Middle East region with a focus on legal technology pilots and implementations, as well as embedding an innovative culture across all practice areas. His initial career background is non-legal, having started in technology consulting at the Big Four in the UK and Argentina, before moving onto innovation roles at two Magic Circle firms, which allowed him a strong grounding in this relatively new field. In his current role he is heavily involved in tangential activities such as practice development, knowledge management, training, business development, and many other aspects of the improvement of legal service delivery in general. Joe read Economics and Spanish at the University of Nottingham and has been shortlisted for various awards in the legal industry, such as Innovation Trailblazer at the Legal Innovation Awards 2021. Under Joe's leadership, in conjunction with his European colleagues, Dentons has placed in the top 10 two years running at the FT Europe innovation awards.

Mark Gediman is a senior research analyst for Alston & Bird, LLP. He is past president of the Southern California Association of Law Libraries as well as co-founder and co-chair of the PLL-IP Competitive Intelligence Caucus. Mark writes and presents regularly on competitive intelligence, research, and library management issues for the American Association of Law Libraries (AALL), California Lawyers Association, Legal Marketing Association (LMA), the Special Libraries Association (SLA), SWALL, SCALL, NoCALL, ACI, and HALL. He contributed to *Business Intelligence for Law Firms* (Ark Group, 2012), *Strategic Intelligence for Law Firms* (Ark Group, 2018), *Innovations in Legal KM* (Ark Group, 2017) and articles in *AALL Spectrum, Practicing Law Management Week, Paralegal Today* and *Facts & Findings – The Magazine of the National Association of Legal Assistants* (NALA). Mark is a graduate of the University of California-Riverside.

Amy Halverson is director of knowledge management, research and information services at Wilson Sonsini Goodrich & Rosati. Amy's team delivers the collective expertise and experience of Wilson Sonsini attorneys, along with strategically sourced legal and business research and information, to each individual attorney in the firm and to its clients. Amy is a graduate of UC Hastings College of the Law and of UCLA. An attorney and former litigator, she initially left private practice to direct the online editorial operations of a national legal news and information website. She then returned to the law firm environment, where she calls upon her legal and technical experience to facilitate the development of tools that capitalize on existing law firm information flows and business processes to advance the firm's business objectives and client service offerings.

Katherine Lang is senior knowledge lawyer for the EMEA real estate team, and London knowledge lead, at international law firm Baker McKenzie. She works with the EMEA real estate management team in aligning cross-jurisdictional thought leadership and business strategy, and advises, writes, and speaks on complex transactional points, legal developments, and their business impact for clients. She is also responsible for coordinating knowledge management across all teams in the London office of the firm. Katherine is a founding member of the Baker McKenzie Knowledge Inclusion and Diversity Committee. Katherine has contributed articles, webinars, and podcasts to various legal and trade publications, including *Estates Gazette* and *Property Week*. She is a member of the editorial board of *Landlord & Tenant Review*, the consulting editorial board of LexisPSL, and the Committee of Oxford Real Estate Society. Katherine has previously worked as a senior knowledge lawyer at a City firm in London, and as a transactional real estate lawyer in London, Dubai, and Abu Dhabi. Katherine began her legal career as a research assistant in the property and trusts law team at the Law Commission for England and Wales. Katherine read geography at St Peter's College, University of Oxford.

James Loft is the COO at Rainbird Technologies, a world-leading low/no-code automation technology. He drives Rainbird's daily business operations and is responsible for the go-to-market focus of the business. With over a decade of experience in leadership positions across innovation, change management, and service design, James is an expert in supporting organizations through successful transformational changes and intelligent automation implementations. Prior to Rainbird, James ran a new technologies consultancy firm and was a key member of a team of senior leaders responsible for innovating and delivering a portfolio of new customer propositions across Barclays bank.

Kevin Miles serves as manager, research services at Norton Rose Fulbright, and co-chairs the AALL PLL-IP Competitive Intelligence Caucus with Mark Gediman. He is past president of the Dallas Association of Law Libraries. Further, he writes a CI column for the AALL Spectrum, and presents CI programs.

Nick Milton is director and co-founder of Knoco Ltd, with over 30 years' experience in knowledge management. Nick has helped develop and deliver KM strategies and services in a wide range of organizations around the globe. He has a particular interest in lesson-learning programs, and has managed major lessons capture programs, particularly in the area of mergers and acquisitions, and high technology engineering. Prior to founding Knoco, Nick spent two years at the center of the team that made BP the leading KM company in the world at the time; acting as the team knowledge manager, developing and implementing BP's knowledge of "how to manage knowledge", and coordinating the BP KM Community of Practice. Nick is the author/co-author of six KM books, including *The Knowledge Manager's Handbook*. He was a member of the international group that developed ISO 30401, the management systems standard for KM, and a co-author of BS 34401, the guide to the standard. He is a widely recognized coach and trainer and has given keynote speeches at most of the leading international KM conferences.

Andrea Miskolczi leads Dentons' European innovation and knowledge management activities. Having 20+ years of experience in the legal business, Andrea is passionate about the change of the legal industry and aims to inspire people to not only embrace, but also to shape, such transformation. In her current role she manages the firm's legal service delivery transformation, LegalTech solution development, and knowledge management across Europe and Central Asia. Prior to joining Dentons, Andrea oversaw innovation and LegalTech, business development and training, as well as marketing and communications at a leading Central and Eastern European law firm. Her understanding of legal services is based on having been a transactional lawyer with one of the Magic Circle law firms in her birth town, Budapest, Hungary. Andrea is a frequent speaker at conferences and one of the best known European thought leaders on the innovation and transformation of legal services. Under Andrea's leadership, in conjunction with her UK colleagues, Dentons has placed in the top 10 two years running at the *Financial Times* Innovative Lawyers Awards. In 2022 she was shortlisted at these awards in the "Change Makers" category.

Tiffany M. O'Neil leads Procopio's knowledge management and records/office services functions while also being responsible for the firm's internal Technology Innovation Group. With over 25 years of experience in KM and research, Tiffany oversees the firm's investigative, business, and legal research, and evaluates and implements KM tools and processes. Tiffany also trains attorneys and staff on efficient research strategies, conducts contract negotiations, budgeting and supervising, and advances the performance of various legal and administrative departments by establishing and implementing valuable workflow solutions. Tiffany is also a member of the firm's Technology Committee. In addition to working in the legal field, Tiffany was an information specialist with McKinsey & Company, a leading management consultant firm.

James G. Perkins, PhD, has for the last 20 years led Procopio's non-legal operations including finance, human resources, administration, marketing and business development, information services, and knowledge management. Jim is a member of the firm's management committee and in 2012 also became the firm's chief compliance officer (CCO) responsible for developing a firm enterprise risk management program. In his CCO capacity he also serves as co-chair, together with the firm's general counsel, of Procopio's office of risk management and compliance. Jim speaks regularly on law firm management issues and business strategy at conferences and international law firm network meetings. He also consults occasionally as part of the Procopio business advisors group.

Tara Pichardo-Angadi leads the knowledge team for the Europe, Middle-East, and Asia region of Norton Rose Fulbright LLP. As head of knowledge for EMEA, her main responsibilities include managing and meeting local stakeholders' knowledge requirements, knowledge plans, developing and sharing best practice, feeding EMEA requirements into the global knowledge strategy, and managing local knowledge teams, including performance reviews, budgets, and projects. Tara is also the knowledge director for training, leading a multi-disciplinary team to create a holistic program of learning for the future of law. Tara regularly assists clients with training requirements, knowledge consulting, and, more generally, helps them access company knowledge.

Dr Anthony J. Rhem, PhD, is a recognized thought leader, author, consultant, and advisor in artificial intelligence, knowledge management, Big Data, information architecture, and innovation. Since 1990, Anthony has served as CEO and principal consultant of AJ Rhem & Associates Inc., a consulting, training, and research firm specializing in KM and AI. As an advisor, Anthony's work includes being a founding editorial board member of *AI and Ethics Journal* by Springer; advisory board member of Halen Technologies, Advisory Board of ABAN Innovations, Inc., former chairman – board of trustees, Knowledge Systems Institute; Industry Advisory Board – International Conference on Software Engineering and Knowledge Engineering (SEKE); Technology Council of Advisors Gerson Lehrman Group (GLG) on Artificial Intelligence and Knowledge Management; former chairman – International Bar Association (IBA) Law Firm Management Committee; and former member of the National Science Foundation SBIR (Small Business Innovative Research) Review Panel in the areas of AI, Blockchain, Internet of Things (IoT), KM, and Education Solutions. As a thought leader, Anthony continues to be an active presenter at AI and KM conferences. In addition, Anthony has written several books and hundreds of articles for trade journals in technology, management, and law including writing in his blog, The Knowledge Management Depot.

Ian Rodwell is head of client knowledge and learning at Linklaters LLP. He provides training and guidance to the firm's clients – global corporates, banks, governments – on an extensive range of business skills topics. These encompass knowledge exploitation, collaboration, high-performing teams, creativity, the role of trust, motivational leadership, hybrid working, influence/impact, and the business use of stories. Ian has delivered master-classes globally and advised clients on the design of offsites, away days, and overarching learning programs. He is also an experienced coach – trained by Lane4 and Moller PSF Group – with assignments both within Linklaters and externally. Ian regularly writes for professional publications on a variety of business topics as well as hosts the Linklaters Ideas Foundry podcast (which explores the changing face of 21st century organizational life). Currently, he is conducting doctoral research on the role of liminal spaces in organizational storytelling.

Kathy Skinner is director of research at White & Case LLP, a global law firm with 45 offices across the world. Kathy leads a 24/7 global function of legal and market researchers and library operations team members located in 23 of the firm's offices. In addition to managing research delivery to support client matters, business development, and firm strategy, the team also provides lawyer research training and manages procurement, budgeting, and vendor relations for research tools and subscriptions. Kathy has led the research function at White & Case since 2017, and her team is part of the business development, knowledge, and marketing function. The research team has been recognized with an FT Innovation Award for its 24/7 service delivery model. Kathy collaborates broadly across the firm to deliver value-added services to clients as part of the firm's client service delivery team. She also works closely with White & Case colleagues on innovation, training, and other projects. Kathy received her MLIS and AB degrees from the University of California at Berkeley.

Jonna Vainikainen is a business process manager and works in the ICT team at Castrén & Snellman Attorneys Ltd in Helsinki. She has a specialist qualification in management and a further vocational qualification in coaching. Jonna's responsibilities include, among other things, business process and master data management, as well as the development of project management. Jonna is actively involved in business development projects and strategy process development and often acts as a project manager in development projects, responsible for leading the project group, scheduling, communications, and training. In addition, she provides induction training and other training for the personnel. Jonna is fascinated by leadership, learning, mental training and development.

Gordon Vala-Webb is a thought leader, speaker/author, and innovation professional. He is a fellow of the College of Law Practice Management with a Master's of Management Science (Technology). With decades of experience leading organizations to become smarter by increasing their flows of information, innovations, and decisions, he put everything he knows into his book, *Building Smarter Organizations: Leading your Zombie Organization Back to Life*. As a consultant, he works with clients like Lex Mundi – a worldwide network of top independent law firms – where he helps their member firms accelerate their uptake of innovative ideas and technology.

Chapter 1:
Knowledge management strategies and frameworks for the post-COVID world

By Nick Milton, director and co-founder, Knoco Ltd

Introduction

The world is coming towards the end of the biggest health crisis for decades, and organizations across the globe are taking stock of the current situation and asking themselves, in a post-pandemic context – "What now?" What new strategies, business models, and approaches will be needed in a post-COVID world? Knowledge managers within those organizations will also be asking themselves similar questions, in order to determine how KM can best support the business in its new endeavors and ways of working. Now is a time for considered reflection, and in this chapter I hope to provide some guidance and models to guide that reflection. I will look at the post-COVID landscape in two dimensions – firstly what new activities and priorities an organization will face, and secondly what new ways of working will be required. The former will set the strategy for KM, while the latter will address the nature of the KM framework itself.

It has to be said at the outset, however, that it is probably premature to conclude the reflection. We are not yet in a post-COVID world; the pandemic is still raging, and though ubiquitous vaccination in the developed world has ended the need for lockdown, there are still large numbers of people either ill or voluntarily self-isolating. It is not yet clear whether the lockdown-enforced pattern of working from home will continue once it is safe to return to the office, whether there will be a hybrid approach mixing home-based and office-based working, or whether, in a year or two, office life will be indistinguishable from office life five years ago. We do not know what will happen, and in that lack of knowledge we can only really look at scenarios.

The four main scenarios

We can consider four possible scenarios for the future of any organization, based on the Boston Square in Figure 1. Each of these scenarios carries risks for KM, and at the same time presents opportunities. The four scenarios are described below.

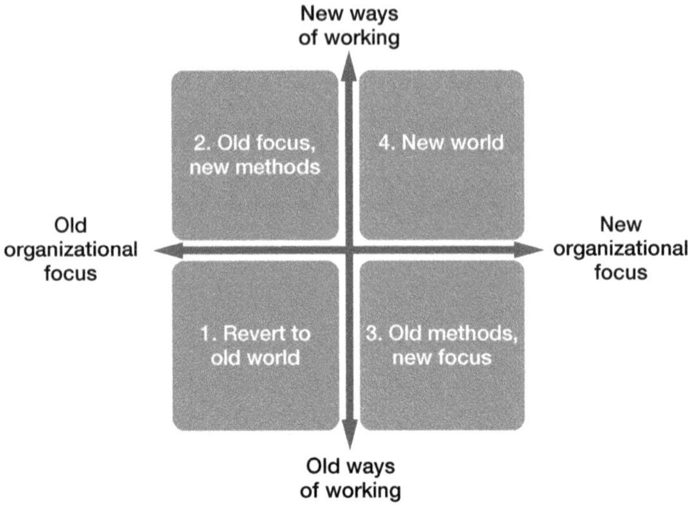

Figure 1: Four possible scenarios.

Scenario 1 – retaining the same organizational focus as before, with the same ways of working

This scenario represents a return to the pre-COVID world. Face-to-face activity and interplay has a freshness and immediacy that Zoom and Teams meetings do not, and remote working does not provide the same opportunities for creativity, innovation, and cross-team knowledge sharing, as discussed later in this chapter. The danger for knowledge management in reverting to the old world is that the gains it made in many organizations, as a facilitator for remote work, may be lost, and reversion to the old world could be a step backward for KM. On the other hand, if the knowledge manager acts quickly, they could build on KM's COVID successes, perhaps by:

- Conducting a learning review of the organization's COVID response to draw out lessons;
- Gathering stories and examples of how KM supported the organization during COVID;
- Making the case that KM can similarly support office-based work; and
- Making the case that KM can also support the transition back to the office.

Scenario 2 – new ways of working with an unchanged organizational focus

This might be, for example, a firm that retains some of the elements of remote or hybrid working, yet the mission and strategy of the organization is the same as it was pre-COVID. For many organizations, KM provided excellent tactical support during COVID, providing help with videoconferencing tools and processes, and helping develop online information repositories. There is a risk that organizations in Scenario 2 may expect KM to continue at this tactical support level, rather than using it as a (more valuable) strategic enabler. The opportunity, on the other hand, is for KM to offer to develop a true hybrid KM framework, which brings creativity, innovation, and cross-team sharing to the hybrid world. Such a framework is discussed later in this chapter.

Scenario 3 – old ways of working, but new organizational focus

The world has moved on during the past few years. Brexit, COVID-19, the "great resignation", hybrid work, the Russian invasion of Ukraine, the energy price shock, the growing influence of climate change – all of these issues can have a profound effect on a business. Perhaps old business lines are no longer viable, while new business lines and business opportunities beckon for fast-moving agile companies. We cannot assume that the post-COVID organizational focus will be the same as the pre-pandemic focus. There is a risk to KM, if it is seen as a tactical rather than a strategic tool, in that it might be ignored when developing new products, services, or business lines. The opportunity, on the other hand, is to make the case that KM is vital to help the organization navigate a new and changing world. KM allows organizations to learn at the speed of change, and to develop and deploy new areas of organizational knowledge. Therefore, a change in organizational focus will require a change in KM strategy, if KM is to deliver on its strategic potential. In several organizations,[1] KM was used to develop and deploy a body of knowledge on "Dealing with COVID". This can be used as a demonstration of KM's ability to help the organization to learn during change, and KM teams should be seeking internal endorsement of the value they brought, in order to gain management endorsement for further strategic support.

Scenario 4 – new ways of working, new organizational focus

This is the "New World" scenario in which the organization will be doing new things, and working in a new way. This is a risky scenario, compounding novelty on novelty, and full commitment to KM will be needed in order to navigate this new world. KM needs a new strategy, to support new areas of focus, and a new framework, to support new ways of working.

In the following sections we discuss first the steps needed to refresh a KM strategy, and then the elements that a new KM framework is likely to need.

KM strategies for a new world

Development of a new, revised, expanded, or updated KM strategy should, nowadays, follow the requirements of the first few clauses of ISO Standard 30401:2018: the Management Systems Standard for Knowledge Management.[2] Whether or not an organization has any plans, or even desire, to seek certification against ISO 30401:2018, the standard still represents the views of the world's leading international standards organization concerning the required components of a management system (and knowledge management is a management system – the management system with knowledge as a focus). Using ISO 30401 to guide strategy development can therefore be claimed to be good practice.

Some of the elements of ISO 30401 are strategic elements, and these are to be found in clauses 4.1, 4.2, and 4.3. Compliance with these clauses ensures that your KM strategy is robust, and requires that you consider the following issues:

- The required outcomes for KM;
- The issues that affect the ability of KM to deliver its outcomes;
- The stakeholders and their needs; and
- The scope of KM, including the critical knowledge topics.

KM outcomes represent the measurable business outcomes that KM will support, which drive the KM strategy, and against which the success of the KM program will be gauged. For some lucky organizations, for whom the post-COVID world is one of opportunity, the required outcome might be growth (sales growth, revenue growth, capacity growth). For others, it might be cost reduction or improved operational efficiency. For others still, it might be capability retention during downsizing (leading to an emphasis on knowledge retention).

The organization should develop a list of **issues** related to this new world, which are either opportunities KM can leverage to deliver the outcomes, or challenges KM may need to surmount. These might be internal issues (new departments, new products, new technology) or external issues (new costs, new competitors, new markets, new demands or constraints). The issue list will start to map out some of the component elements of the strategy, and will flow down into operational KM plans.

The **stakeholders** for KM may be the same as in the pre-COVID world, or there may be significant changes to the list. However, the needs of these stakeholders are likely to have changed, and the KM team should canvas them to understand their new needs. These stakeholders include the users of the KM framework (e.g., the knowledge workers who will use the framework to gain the knowledge they need to do their job), and also those with an interest in the outcomes, such as senior management and external customers. Prioritize this list; you may not be able to satisfy all stakeholders equally.

The **scope** of KM may have changed[3] during the pandemic, and KM may have expanded (or contracted) both its remit and its organizational reach. The extent of this scope needs to be determined for the post-COVID world.

In addition, the scope should be redefined in terms of **critical knowledge**. New organizational activities need to be supported by new knowledge, and in scenarios three and four above, the KM team will need to define and agree a new prioritized list of critical knowledge topics that will represent its prioritized areas of focus.

Together, the new outcomes, issues, stakeholders and their needs, scope and critical knowledge form the foundation for a new KM strategy. This strategy will be delivered through a KM framework, which may or may not need to be updated for post-COVID ways of working.

How KM operated during lockdown and remote working

In scenarios two and four above, organizations will be operating with new ways of working, some of which may be extensions of patterns developed during lockdown. The KM framework needs to adapt to these new ways of working. Many commentators believe that many approaches to working from home (WFH) will persist, and that organizations may adopt a hybrid model in future, mixing office-based and home-based work. Of course, as mentioned in the introduction, that may not be the case, and perhaps within two years office work will be the norm again. However, if hybrid work and WFH are to be more common, then it is useful to see how KM operated during lockdown, in order for the new KM framework to build on the strengths and address the weaknesses.

Respondents to a 2021 survey of changes to KM due to lockdown[4] suggested that WFH and remote working created the following positive effects (in the words of selected survey respondents):

- Greater access to, and participation from, remote offices;
- Cost and time savings for meetings;
- More accessible data due to remote working;
- More habitual online collaboration;
- People are more focused and the requirement to capture and share (knowledge) has been greatly enhanced;
- It became easier to conduct sessions with people from multiple geographies; and
- The needs from the business have become more clear. As a result, KM in all its facets has become a bigger priority for management and more space for new KM projects has been made available.

In addition, the following negative effects were reported:

- You have to make an effort to contact people. Juniors are not learning by overhearing conversations;
- Less ad-hoc knowledge sharing from employees;
- More difficult to effectively engage with people;
- Personal knowledge sharing has been impacted;
- Our interviews are now more difficult to do. Also, the possibility to use physical billboards (knowledge walls) has been limited because half of the people don't appear in the office;
- Training (especially for new joiners) was harder;
- The inability to have random, face-to-face contacts between those of us working (with KM) as well as others within the organization who may champion the initiative has been problematic; and
- While overall remote work has been good, lack of direct interaction and a focus on more "formalized" approaches to reaching out to one another (e.g., scheduled meetings) feels like it has had a negative impact on our reach.

In summary, KM during lockdown supported remote collaboration between team members, and the requirement for KM became more obvious to management and staff alike. At the same time, the richness of face-to-face communication, and unplanned ad-hoc knowledge gathering and sharing, were lost.

Other studies have shown similar results. An article entitled "The effects of remote work on collaboration among information workers", published in *Nature* in 2021 by Yang et al,[5] looked at the working habits of over 60,000 US Microsoft employees before and after the pandemic, to study how work habits shifted as working became remote. There are several very interesting conclusions from this article. One came from an analysis of how the number of "ties" changed as remote working was introduced – ties being organizational connections which are either strong (regular interaction), weak (occasional interaction), or bridging (interaction with someone in a different division or team). Strong ties are often found between members of a work team, while bridging ties and weak ties are one of the primary ways in which knowledge flows from group to group, division to division, and project to project. The study demonstrated clearly that time spent with weak, cross-group, new (added), or bridging ties dropped significantly as workers moved to remote working. One of the conclusions of the study was the following:

> *"Our results suggest that shifting to firm-wide remote work caused the collaboration network to become more heavily siloed – with fewer ties that cut across formal business units or bridge structural holes in Microsoft's informal collaboration network – and that those silos became more densely connected. Furthermore, the network became more static, with fewer ties added and deleted per month. Previous research suggests that these changes in collaboration patterns may impede the transfer of knowledge and reduce the quality of workers' output."*

Nancy Dixon, in a 2022 blog post entitled "Where Is The Only Place Employees Share Their Knowledge? The Hallways of Learning"[6] uses the analogy of hallways as silo-bridging locations or processes where knowledge is shared. She cites conferences, where the richest knowledge is shared not in the formal lectures in conference rooms, but in the informal hallway conversations. Organizations can set up processes and structures, such as Communities of Practice or Peer Assist, to provide this "hallway" function, as Dixon claims that "Hallways are the only space where it is possible for an organization to learn". However, the results of the Microsoft study show that in the world of remote work, although the online team rooms work well for collaboration between "strong ties", the hallways are becoming deserted.

Remote working, and by extension hybrid working, therefore brings risks of more siloed teams, less knowledge sharing between weak ties, and fewer hallway-based knowledge sharing across teams. It brings risks of more communication on tasks and actions, and less communication of knowledge. It brings significant risk to effective knowledge management.

A KM framework for a hybrid organization

If, in the new world scenarios two and four, organizations will work in a different way, including much more common remote and hybrid working, then the KM framework must be strengthened to ensure that the silos are breached, the "hallway" spaces and processes are deliberately and actively applied, and that interactions between weak and bridging ties become built into the patterns of work. A hybrid organization can no longer rely on ad-hoc knowledge sharing, overheard conversations, or chance encounters in real hallways, at water coolers, or around the tea kettle. Knowledge management must ensure that the flow of knowledge becomes intentional and planned, through the adoption of roles, processes, and structures as part of a management system for KM.

Unfortunately, there is no long history of knowledge sharing in remote and hybrid organizations, as this is a relatively recent development (at least on the scale that we see in early 2022), and there is therefore no current best practice model for KM in such a context. Possibly the most useful model we can look at is the multinationals, or organizations with many branch offices, where KM has had to deal with people working remotely from each other in a geographic sense. In many ways, with modern remote working, everyone is their own site office, so how do organizations with multiple site offices manage knowledge?

The management framework such organizations use for KM tends to work as follows:

- To cross the silos, and to build the "bridging ties", a set of Communities of Practice (CoPs) is defined, each one covering an area of practice that cross-cuts the team/division structure. In a hybrid world, these communities need their own communication channels, as well as their own roles, processes, and governance. Each community lives in its own hallway.
- These communities act as mutual help groups, helping members find knowledge and experience to solve their problems, and most of the traffic in the CoPs is driven by problems and questions.
- These CoPs are recognized organizational entities, with specific and dedicated roles.

- There is a pervasive culture, supported, modelled, and specifically expected by management, that people will use the knowledge of the CoP in solving any problem.
- Work projects may start with a knowledge gap analysis session, which prompts people to reach out to their CoPs and weak ties. The project leader needs to intentionally ask their team: "Who else can we learn from?" This question forces them to look outside team space, to look through the windows in the walls, to look into the hallways to see who else has valuable knowledge. And then they track those conversations to make sure the knowledge is brought into the team space, perhaps through Peer Assist or another process.
- The CoPs work asynchronously as well as synchronously; through question-driven online forums backed up where needed by richer real-time conversations.
- The CoPs take a major role in validating and stewarding the organizational knowledge base for their practice area.
- Often there is an expertise locator in the organization, where you can search for people by knowledge topic, and so staff can find others, outside their current circle of contacts (added ties) who can share knowledge to help solve problems.
- Work projects include activities for discussion of knowledge, such as Retrospects, After Action Reviews, Peer Assist etc., which not only drive knowledge sharing within the project team, but also help people become conscious of what they have learned, and which other teams they need to share this with. Again, this forces the team to look through the walls and into the hallways.

None of the above is new. However, in a hybrid world, such elements of KM, borrowed from the multinationals and adapted to other organizations, will be crucial in ensuring that remote working does not impede the flow of knowledge.

Conclusions

We do not yet know what the post-COVID world will look like, nor do we yet know the role KM will play in that world. However, we can look at at least four main scenarios. Some scenarios involve the organization addressing new issues and possibilities in the post-COVID world, and KM will need to adapt and renew its strategy in response. The early clauses in

ISO 30401:2018 provide useful guidance for this strategic review. Other scenarios involve the organization working in a different way, perhaps with a greater level of remote or hybrid working. Here a new KM framework will be needed, with significant attention and intentionality paid to the need to breach team silos that otherwise may be strengthened as people interact remotely. The KM frameworks used by multinationals, where teams are globally remote, can be used as inspiration for KM in a hybrid organization.

Whichever scenario turns out to be closest to reality, the post-COVID world represents a time of both risk and opportunity for KM and the KM professional. If we can take the learning and the credit gained during the pandemic and use these to make the case for KM as strategic business support, then the future is bright both for the KM discipline and the organizations it serves.

References

1 14 percent of respondents to a 2021 survey said their KM had helped the organization by developing knowledge of the organizational COVID response. The survey is available free of charge from www.knoco.com/knowledge-management-survey.htm.

2 ISO (2018) *Knowledge management systems – requirements* – ISO 30401:2018, ISO, Geneva.

3 In a 2021 survey, 69 percent of respondents said that new work items had needed to be added to KM during COVID-19, with only 23 percent saying old work items had been removed. www.knoco.com/knowledge-management-survey.htm

4 www.knoco.com/knowledge-management-survey.htm

5 Yang, L., Holtz, D., Jaffe, S. et al. "The effects of remote work on collaboration among information workers". Nat Hum Behav 6, 43–54 (2022). https://doi.org/10.1038/s41562-021-01196-4

6 www.nancydixonblog.com/2022/04/where-is-the-only-place-employees-share-their-knowledge.html

Chapter 2:
Adapting legal knowledge management to the hybrid workplace

By Chris Boyd, chief operating officer, and Amy Halverson, director of knowledge management, research and information services, Wilson Sonsini Goodrich & Rosati

Introduction

The post-pandemic practice of law will primarily be a hybrid one, with some work being done collaboratively in the office and other work (perhaps most work) done at home or another non-office location. That is a big change from the pre-pandemic norm of most work being done in the office. The abrupt shift to remote work forced legal knowledge management (KM) professionals quickly to adapt practices and workflows to meet the needs of attorneys and clients working from home all the time. Law firms that had established KM programs in place before the pandemic found that KM practices such as just-in-time content delivery, targeted communications, and resource training proved foundational to the transition to fully remote work.

In this chapter, we describe the reasons that law firms will likely move to a hybrid work setup that optimizes the balance of in-office and remote work. We then examine ways in which law firm KM programs successfully navigated the move to fully remote work, and how those strategies can be leveraged to get the greatest returns from KM in a hybrid work environment.

The new legal workplace will be a hybrid one

The pandemic has taught us that, with narrow exceptions such as jury trials, law can be practiced remotely and lawyers can be highly effective while working from home or other non-office locations. There are many benefits to employees working from home, including:

1. *Flexibility and convenience.* Employees can take the time they would have spent getting ready for the office and commuting to it, and instead spend it on their personal life. They can avoid the chore of packing

things up and lugging them around. Employees with children can see them more and have much more freedom to take them to places they need to be. Employees can use down time at home to walk their dogs, exercise, do laundry, and take care of other home tasks.

2. *Cost savings and lower environmental footprint.* In addition to saving significant money on commuting expenses, employees can make lunches at home rather than buying them at work. Cutting out some or all of the commute has also reduced each employee's carbon emissions, consumption of packaged goods, and other environmental footprints.
3. *Ability to work from multiple locations.* Employees who can work completely remotely have the flexibility to work anywhere, including the ability to travel around and visit family, friends, and locations of interest. Such employees can also access a much wider range of potential employers and jobs.
4. *Potentially stronger work ties.* Perhaps counterintuitively, working from home can help strengthen professional ties with colleagues. Employees can work on cases, deals, or other matters with a broader group of supervisors, including ones in other offices. The move to videoconferencing has created much more face-to-face interaction, even if virtual. Colleagues seem more real when they're dressed in casual clothes and have their homes in the backgrounds of their Zoom screens. Finally, in many cases, junior associates are more often included in online chats and videoconferences that they wouldn't have previously and are thereby learning more.

While there are many benefits to working from home, there are also many benefits to collaborating together in the office, including:

1. *Stronger professional and career development.* Working in the office tends to provide more in-person training and feedback for junior associates and staff. Meeting in person tends to generate a lot more conversation and interaction, including before and after the formal meeting agenda. It's also easier for junior lawyers and staff to ask in-person questions of supervisors.
2. *Stronger teams and culture.* Working together in the office generally leads to better integration of new employees. It's also easier to build professional relationships through social interactions afforded by coffees, lunches, and other physical co-presence. Working together in

meetings and offices enables people to observe the dynamic and interpersonal relationships within their teams. Finally, just being together in the same hallway, wing, or floor provides many more informal and impromptu opportunities to check in on colleagues, connect with them, and reduce isolation.

3. *Clearer work–life boundaries.* Going to and from the office, and more clearly delineating between the office/work "space" and home "space" also seems to define clearer boundaries between work time and home time. Our lawyers have reported that clients seem to respect business hours more when everyone is in the office than when everyone is working from home.
4. *Convenience of office environment and services.* Working in the office provides access to generally superior document printing, internet access, IT support, climate control and lighting, and other office services.

Given the substantial advantages of both working from home and working in the office, law firms and other employers will likely institutionalize a hybrid work setup that offers lawyers and professional staff the optimal balance of in-office and at-home work. Law firms that strike the best balance will attract and retain the strongest performers while also providing the most value to clients and professional and career development opportunities for their people.

Law firms have been exploring different types of hybrid work arrangements. Some firms have been asking all employees to come in on specific days, such as Tuesday, Wednesday, and Thursday. Others have said that they expect lawyers to come in two to three days a week and left it up to the lawyers to decide which days to come in. Still others have promised complete flexibility and autonomy, although anecdotal reports indicate that in reality partners expect lawyers to come in at least half of the time.

Our firm decided to leave it up to each organic workgroup to decide (a) how many days to come in each week, (b) which weekday(s) they would come in, and (c) what collaborative group activities they would do together to capture the advantages of physical co-presence described above. After a few months of using this system, most groups are coming in one or two days per week and hosting a team lunch one day (which the firm pays for). The team lunch topics include general catch-up and conversation, matter updates, developments in law and practice, and practical tips. Importantly, we have encouraged the groups to be flexible and allow team members to come in more or less than the hybrid norm as individual circumstances warrant. We believe this approach best balances the advantages of collaborating in the office and flexibly working from home, and the feedback so far confirms that belief.

KM resources and practices will be key to making the hybrid workplace succeed

Many law firm KM programs had set up processes before the pandemic that supported the swift and forced transition to fully remote work. KM teams were able to leverage just-in-time online content delivery, targeted communications, and personalized training, each of which were essential to enabling the move to fully remote work. These processes will continue to be critical components of a successful KM program under hybrid work.

Just-in-time content delivery

For years prior to the pandemic, legal knowledge management professionals worked toward the goal of "just-in-time" delivery of know-how to attorneys – the idea being that attorneys should not have to canvass all knowledge resources to find the specific thing needed. Instead, the KM professional should smooth the path by aligning KM forms to legal workflows, so that as an attorney progressed through a transaction or other matter, they could find the next KM asset easily because it was associated with the immediate phase or task.

To achieve this goal, many KM teams organized knowledge resources not only around practice areas, but also around matter workflows. For example, when incorporating a start-up company, employment agreements are typically also needed – so KM worked those forms in with the incorporation forms. For some types of matters, the precedent forms were built into automation platforms, so the attorney did not even need to leave the online questionnaire to use the full set of forms.

Most KM teams long ago learned to build and maintain intranet content systems themselves, so they can now update and edit content quickly as needs arise and as new precedent and instructional materials are generated. Our firm's KM team uses SharePoint, simple HTML pages, the firm's enterprise search tool, and the firm's document management system to make KM resources available to attorneys 24-7. This ability to publish and push out content autonomously proved invaluable during the pandemic.

Transitioning to delivery... from a distance

The sudden shift to fully remote work meant that KM and the library needed to deliver content to attorneys where they physically were – online, at home, in various time zones. Our KM and research team immediately shifted to Microsoft Teams as a means not only of providing outreach via status buttons, messaging, and calls, but as a content delivery platform, in addition to bolstering KM intranet content.

The firm decided to set up an internal COVID-19 resource center to aggregate multidisciplinary guidance for the firm's clients. KM published one quickly using SharePoint and then used Teams to set up SharePoint portals for attorney working groups, and enabled those groups to publish and update their Teams resources directly, with no publishing bottlenecks. KM also helped practice groups launch their own internal e-newsletters that allowed attorneys to share updates and developments of note without having in-person group meetings.

Document automation became even more desirable in the fully remote environment, as an automated suite of forms provides a universal source of reference to attorney teams. KM expanded the breadth of the firm's portfolio of automated corporate documents in response to attorney demand, and is exploring a broader self-automation program whereby anyone at the firm can automate documents, including those in administrative departments and legal support.

Targeted communications and training

KM professionals learned through painful experience that getting attorneys to use KM resources and tools is more challenging than acquiring the tools in the first place. Without a marketing and training program, KM content and practice technology will sit unused.

Our KM and research team had already developed a program of targeted communications to all new hires, to encourage users to incorporate KM into their workflows early on. We developed several different email templates, with each one catered to a specific practice area and role. We send these out to individual new hires two weeks after their start dates. The emails provide links to resources tailored to the new hire's practice along with targeted online training sessions. These have proven to be far more effective than pre-pandemic trainings, which were typically held in a conference room with a live video feed for remote participants; virtual attendees were not visible to the conference room attendees, and remote attendees rarely asked questions.

Connecting through one-on-one conversations and converting in-print users to online resources

KM had always offered one-on-one training to new hires on KM tools, usually with only modest uptake. However, once the firm moved to completely virtual new employee onboarding, the positive response rate more than doubled. KM and the library were able to use short Teams meetings to make personal, one-on-one connections with a materially higher proportion of the firm's new attorneys and staff, in addition to the group orientations for new hires. We used Teams instant messaging for instantaneous, in-the-moment Q&As, and when appropriate turned on our cameras when having phone conversations.

As attorneys left reference books and manuals in the office and turned to online research and information resources, the library rolled out targeted virtual trainings to practice groups, with an initial emphasis on how to use online versions of materials that historically were used in print. The team built a catalog of searchable resource landing pages on the intranet, and customized lists of resources for different practices. Working with the firm's vendors and IT department, we shifted as many subscription products as possible onto single-sign-on protocols, which enable users to log into subscription products without the entry of dedicated usernames and passwords, thereby providing attorneys with seamless access to licensed resources.

The department began giving office managers monthly updates on KM and library training sessions, new resources and procedures, so that they could incorporate them into their own office-specific communications to attorneys and staff.

Preparing KM for a hybrid future by cultivating connections

The initial shift to online, remote work caused many law firm KM and research departments to bolster their collections of written know-how – forms, samples, guides, checklists, research memos and the like – to meet the needs of a fully remote workforce. These efforts strengthened the KM team's relationships with those attorneys and staff who were already known to be content contributors. Without informal office visits, however, group lunches and hallway conversations, connections between acquaintances – much less entirely new employees – diminished. The once steady, if anecdotal, source of news relating to client projects, attorney needs, and legal developments began to fade.

To make up for that loss, many KM teams need to be more deliberate in fostering connections with practice group and department "ambassadors" in order to gain visibility into attorney and client needs. Practice group meetings are a good source of information, to the extent they are organized and available for KM to attend. Some large US-based law firms are addressing the need by staffing practice support lawyers (PSLs) who either formally or informally report into KM and act as a conduit of information between the practice and KM, and also as pipeline of KM content.

A less deliberate approach of reproducing those serendipitous communications, used by organizers of virtual conferences and large group online meetings, is the "breakout rooms" enabled with the conference platform. These randomly assign attendees into smaller groups and can enable introductions to people one may not have met before, and set up opportunities for follow-up contact.

Leveraging fully remote learnings to optimize KM for a hybrid world

Because a hybrid work environment best balances the advantages of in-person and remote work, law firms will largely embrace hybrid as their standard work model. Law firm KM teams should adapt their content, training, and relationship-building to such a setup, and can use lessons learned during the past two years of fully remote work to optimize their offerings accordingly. Our firm has benefitted greatly from these adaptations, including just-in-time content delivery, virtual collaboration, targeted marketing and training, and cultivated connections, and we are leveraging these as we move into a hybrid work world.

Chapter 3:
Social KM in a time of COVID... and beyond

By Ian Rodwell, head of client knowledge and learning, Linklaters LLP

The role of social KM

For anyone wishing to understand the blend of behaviors, processes, and systems that underpin the discipline of knowledge management (KM), *Knowledge management systems – requirements* (International Standard – ISO 30401) provides an excellent starting point. Its strength derives from the breadth and scope of its KM definition. KM is not restricted to collating and exploiting the knowledge embedded in documents, emails, and web pages. More expansively, it "focuses on managing the working environment, thus nurturing the knowledge lifecycle".[1] Such a wide-ranging conceptualization brings a complex mix of considerations into the KM fold – interpersonal and spatial dynamics, the nature of communication, and organizational culture. This is given practical application in the "knowledge spectrum" that comprises Annex A of the Standard.

Drawing on Nonaka and Takeuchi's theory[2] of tacit and explicit knowledge (which, in turn, links back to Polyani's assertion that "we can know more than we can tell"),[3] ISO 30401 presents KM as a continuum. At one end, we find uncodified knowledge – the deeply embedded insights and experience that we may not even know we possess – and which emerges through judgment calls and intuition. At the other, we have recorded, codified, and documented knowledge (in a law firm, for example, the library of precedents, checklists, templates, and good/best practice). Consequently, KM emerges as a series of transitional activities from *personal reflection/observation* to *encouraging conversations* (the knowledge that emerges and is transferred via stories, conversations, and even gossip) to *managing content* (which brings in questions of taxonomies, structuring, search, AI exploitation etc.) to diffusing and leveraging the value of the knowledge generated.

In my own professional field (that of law firms), formal KM activities are often centered on the capture and exploitation of codified knowledge assets. Yet, a vast amount of knowledge is created and exchanged via discourse and observation. It happens countless times every day, but often without us being aware that such knowledge generation is taking place. For example, a junior lawyer overhearing a telephone conversation where a partner is trying to reassure a worried client may learn – through the partner's words, the tone or rhythm of their responses, and the degree of empathy/understanding they exhibit – how best (or not!) to handle such an interaction. Such osmotic learning[4] may happen without conscious understanding or awareness. But the mundane "naturalness" of these occurrences should not dilute their value.

Let's also consider two colleagues bumping into each other by the lifts – a random, serendipitous encounter. Maybe they discuss what they've been working on, unpick a problem or issue that's concerning them, or perhaps one of them just needs to vent: "You'll never believe what X has just gone and done…". Although seemingly unremarkable, such arbitrary "gatherings and paths crossings"[5] are important in facilitating the flow of knowledge and ideas across diverse organizational populations, thus leading to increased innovation, creativity, and problem-solving.[6]

We might refer to this aspect of knowledge activity as social KM. Knowledge creation that emerges via the direct interaction of individuals (scheduled or unplanned). Some of these exchanges will be more formal. Think of knowhow updates in meetings, the conversations within communities of practice (CoPs), or structured KM interventions such as pre-mortems, peer assists, or after-action-reviews. Others comprise what I term "KM in the wild" – knowledge that emerges through informal, random, or serendipitous exchanges. More often than not, these interactions will involve short, informal stories – "so what happened then was…". Indeed, there is a rich seam of research on organizational storytelling, originating in the 1970s,[7] and my own doctoral investigations have confirmed the valuable work that stories perform. They act as valuable sense-making and sense-giving tools capable of representing complex data and relationships and transmitting context-rich knowledge. More particularly, my own research respondents spoke about how stories helped them gain fresh perspectives on challenges, avoid previous mistakes, or recycle successes from the past, understand the organizational culture better, spark innovative ideas or solutions, "get things off their chest", and build relationships and social capital. They observed that stories enabled them to understand their colleagues better, to see beyond the "mask", and reflected on how this "rounded picture" could enhance team performance.

Yet, with the emergence of COVID-19 and the subsequent shift across the world to remote working (where possible), what were the consequences for social KM? As a form of exchange often reliant on face-to-face interaction and co-location with colleagues, how would it fare as our primary channels of communication became Zoom, Teams, Jabber, and WebEx? Also, what would happen to stories in this new workplace environment – would they migrate seamlessly to new, online habitats or would their survival be under threat?

The impact of COVID-19 on social KM

In the summer of 2020, I participated in a Thomson Reuters Legal Insights Europe webinar that discussed the interplay of KM and change management in law firms.[8] As panelists we all agreed on the role KM had played in helping our organizations work seamlessly during the early days of lockdown and beyond. Our investment in KM systems to organize our codified knowledge assets – the intranets, knowledge databases, search technologies, wiki pages, document management systems etc., as well as the teams that built and supported them – ensured that our dispersed lawyers had efficient access to the knowhow that enabled uninterrupted support to their clients. Similarly, the experience developed in sharing and creating knowledge in response to fast-moving legal and regulatory developments now enabled us to promptly gather and re-circulate emergent good practice on how to work as complex, global, and entirely remote teams. As different regions and offices experienced lockdowns, pragmatic guidance on how best to conduct meetings virtually, train and develop colleagues, and retain morale and motivation in a volatile and uncertain environment were collated and shared across our respective networks.

But – and this was a big "but" – what was happening to KM "out in the wild"? From the workshops I was running with colleagues and clients on different aspects of remote working, some consistent themes began to emerge. While recognizing many benefits of working from home – more time with the family, no commute, fewer interruptions/greater focus – participants identified several key concerns.

A key challenge was, to borrow a term from Luciano Floridi, "information friction".[9] Suddenly, we were deprived of the information gained as a coincidental consequence of being co-located. For example, lawyers told me how delegating work had become more time-consuming and problematic. In the office, having instructed a junior lawyer on a particular task, you might later wander past their desk and just from their look, their posture, learn whether they were struggling or not. Working remotely, that immediate information source was denied. Of course, you could call or message your colleague but that required intent and deliberation. In addition, would the information you receive be as truthful, undisguised, or transparent?

A further consequence of this information friction was a potential erosion of social capital. Colleagues spoke of "feeling disconnected", "out of the flow". Often, I feel, this social capital accumulates through small, mundane, workplace rituals that teams and groups develop – cakes on a Thursday afternoon, a lunchtime run on a Friday, a group lunch on someone's birthday. I was intrigued by how quickly – and spontaneously – colleagues instigated their own replacement rituals during lockdown (I suspect many of us experienced the proliferation – and often short duration – of virtual tea parties, drinks, quizzes, game nights etc.).

Similarly, questions quickly surfaced about the reduced opportunities for osmotic learning. This was often the by-product of people being in the same place at the same time with opportunities for observing and overhearing. Other than being on a continual conference call with colleagues, how were junior lawyers now able to gain exposure to such conversations? This was exacerbated for those joining organizations during lockdown. I recall a discussion with a client in which we reflected on how you can *truly* gain an understanding of the culture of an organization remotely. If culture is, in essence, how we "do things around here" – the values, normative behavior, beliefs, and stories of a particular group – what happens if your view of "what is done around here" is only very partial? For example, it becomes more difficult, as a new joiner, to work out the personalities, working styles, and dynamics of the team around you.

The final concern was the loss of serendipity. A few weeks into lockdown, colleagues and clients observed how they were missing the chance encounters and random "collisions" in their workplace corridors, lifts, staircases, kitchens, and cafes. Around the same time, numerous articles, podcasts, and blog posts referenced the absence of those "spontaneous conversations... that have led to greater insight and better ideas".[10] Even Andy Haldane, the then chief economist at the Bank of England, lamented the loss of informal, spontaneous face-to-face encounters that enable the sharing of "tacit knowledge" and form the "bedrock of relationship-building".[11] Such serendipity is the "cradle of creativity".[12] As many of us found, such randomness was almost impossible to simulate via conferencing platforms where interactions are scheduled between known participants. These are spaces that embody precision and deliberation rather than chance and informality.

Slowly, but surely, we found solutions and social KM began to re-appear in the virtual workplace. For example, informal social media tools (such as Yammer) enabled our team to dip in and out of virtual conversations (some work-related, some not) and retain a sense of cohesion and "being part of something". Similarly, weekly videos by senior leaders provided continuity and connection. Many of those ideas and approaches are still relevant as we enter a COVID-emergent world – a world where many organizations have adopted hybrid working practices (a flexible blend of co-located and virtual working).

"Rewilding" social KM in a COVID-emergent world

So, in the COVID emergent organization, what practical steps can we take to "rewild" KM – to ensure that knowledge exchange and creation through observation, reflection, and discourse flourishes in the new world of hybrid working?

Drawing on discussions with colleagues and clients across multiple organizations and the ideas they implemented, here are three approaches to consider in your own organizations. The theme that connects them is deliberation and intent. In a hybrid workplace, what formerly happened naturally and spontaneously may now require more thoughtful, purposeful, yet gentle orchestration.

Protect the liminal pause

In a wonderful blog post, Paul Gilbert talks about the magic and power of the "liminal pause" – those moments before and after a meeting as people pour their coffee or pack their bags, and talk informally, about holidays, weekends, life "outside the agenda".[13] Gilbert argues that such moments are vital in building connection, understanding, and empathy, yet so often they became a casualty in the rush to Zoom and Team calls. Now, in a world where some attendees may be together in a room and others dialing in, we should continue to make time and space for such exchanges (and ensure that those attending remotely are included!). As the chair of a meeting or catch-up, encourage those conversations, don't curtail them in a rush to start the agenda or move on to the next meeting. It may seem a trite or minor thing to do but these small actions to re-establish connection are fundamental in creating the collaborative environment in which more business-related knowledge can flow.

Cultivate serendipity

There is much current debate on those tasks best suited to working remotely and those which realize their benefits through co-location. One idea is to use time in the office to take advantage of spontaneous and random encounters. So, rather than use office time for endless calls or meetings, think about how you can cultivate serendipity. Maybe go for a walk down the corridor, spend time in the public spaces (café areas, canteens), perhaps work in a different spot? Over the years, I have heard several anecdotes from teams relocated to spaces with a high footfall (near to the toilets, kitchen, or next to a "play" area) and, although busy and noisy, they spoke enthusiastically about how such locations brought them into contact with people they had never met before. Such encounters deliver tangible benefits. One legal team explained that as colleagues got to know them (as trust and social capital accumulated), they would pre-emptively raise questions and issues before they turned into problems. At an organizational level, think about stimulating serendipity through activities such as "randomized coffee trials" – randomly assigned coffee catch-ups that match people across functions, hierarchies, and roles. Such encounters provide opportunities to share thoughts, ideas, and perspectives across the intangible boundaries that crisscross our organizations. Consequently, this cross-pollination facilitates what Matthew Syed terms cognitive diversity[14] and the emergence of fresh thinking, creative ideas, and innovation.

Facilitate osmosis

In maximizing the opportunities for osmotic learning, I have seen various approaches adopted. Some teams have suggested "anchor days"[15] to ensure that junior and more senior members are in the workplace at the same time (exhortations for juniors to spend more time in the office are counter-productive if those they might learn from are absent!). Co-location also makes it easier for informal, spur of the moment questions ("Can I have a quick word about this matter", "I just want to check... when you said..."). In contrast, some colleagues noted that remote working made such ad hoc check-ins more problematic. In the office, it is relatively easy to see if someone is available/not too busy – online, that awareness is more difficult to establish. Although it is very easy to send an email, text message, or call, some juniors expressed concern that this might be experienced as intrusive or annoying.[16]

When working apart, greater deliberation is required to ensure that opportunities for learning are maximized. Colleagues spoke about the necessity of ensuring cameras are switched on when delegating remotely – "it's not perfect, but I have a greater chance of picking up from their body language, whether the brief is understood or not". Similarly, others spoke about re-creating those informal debriefs that might naturally occur following a meeting with a client or a conference call – either walking back along the corridor or going off to get a coffee and chatting about what had happened. These micro after-action reviews provide an excellent "teachable moment" – an opportunity to explore "What did you learn from that?", "Did anything surprise or intrigue you about what was discussed?", "Is there anything you'd like me to explain?". Remotely, such conversations are, of course, still possible but they require more formality and deliberation – maybe staying on the Teams call after everyone else has left or setting up a separate call/chat soon afterwards.

Concluding thoughts

The shape and function of the workplace in a COVID-emergent world has attracted (and continues to attract) much discussion. Is hybrid working a temporary "blip" or merely the first step in a radical re-configuration of how we collaborate, innovate together, learn, form connections, build and inculcate culture? My own view is that the genie is well and truly out of the bottle and increasingly reluctant to return. This gives us an opportunity to re-think the spaces in which we work – both material and virtual – and encourage an "ecology" that develops multiple ways of creating and transmitting knowledge. Remember that definition from ISO 30401 we started with? KM is concerned with "managing the working environment" – and I believe we should construe "environment" literally, not metaphorically.

As with all stories, there is no single narrative. In the preliminary findings from my own research – where my respondents talk about their storytelling spaces during COVID and beyond – some have adapted to a fertile, virtual environment of WhatsApp, Zoom, and Teams while others mourn their "sad", "empty" offices and the arid knowledge deserts they claim have subsequently evolved.

The future of social KM is, it seems, still precariously in the balance. It is therefore crucial that we take every opportunity to purposefully "rewild" our workplaces and thereby stimulate connection and knowledge exchange. Let's defy the encroaching desert and see what oases we can build!

References

1 International Organization for Standardization (2018) ISO 30401:2018 (E) *Knowledge management systems – requirements*. Geneva: ISO, p. vi. See also Collison, C., Corney, P.J., and Eng, P.L. (2019) *The KM cookbook: stories and strategies for organisations exploring knowledge management standard ISO 30401*, London: Facet Publishing for a highly insightful and pragmatic exploration of the standard.

2 Nonaka, I. (1991) "The knowledge-creating company", *Harvard Business Review*, 69(6), pp. 96-104; Nonaka, I. and Takeuchi, H. (1995) *The knowledge-creating*

company: how Japanese companies create the dynamics of innovation. Oxford: Oxford University Press.

3 Polyani, M. (1966) *The tacit dimension*. New York: Doubleday, p4.

4 For a fascinating early description of this term, see Eno, B. (2020) *A year with swollen appendices: Brian Eno's diary* (25th anniversary edition) London: Faber & Faber, p30.

5 A beautifully poetic phrase used by one of my research respondents.

6 See Allen, T. J. (1977) *Managing the flow of information*. Cambridge, Mass.: MIT Press; Kornberger, M. and Clegg, S. R. (2004) "Bringing space back in: organizing the generative building", *Organization Studies*, 25(7), pp. 1,095-1,114; and Dibble, R. and Gibson, C. B. (2018) "Crossing team boundaries: a theoretical model of team boundary permeability and a discussion of why it matters", *Human Relations*, 71(7), pp. 925-950.

7 See e.g., Mitroff, R. and Kilmann, I. (1975) "Stories managers tell: a new tool for organizational problem solving", *Management Review*, July, pp.18-28.

8 *The key to technology adoption is in your law firm's culture* – https://legalsolutions.thomsonreuters.co.uk/blog/2020/07/22/the-key-to-technology-adoption-is-in-your-law-firms-culture/.

9 Floridi, L. (2014) *The fourth revolution: how the infosphere is reshaping human reality*. Oxford: Oxford University Press, pp.103-105.

10 McFarland, J. (2020) "Wellness in the workplace: missing connections with colleagues", *Workplace Design Magazine*. www.workdesign.com/2020/09/wellness-in-the-workplace-missing-connections-with-colleagues

11 Haldane, A. (2020) "Is home working good for you?" www.bankofengland.co.uk/-/media/boe/files/speech/2020/is-home-working-good-for-you-speech-by-andy-haldane.pdf?la=en&hash=099975AB9B41135F1DC132D90C5466DDD4598218

12 *Ibid.*

13 Gilbert, P. (2020) "When the meeting ends," www.lbcwisecounsel.com/resources/articles/article/when-the-meeting-ends/#.Ysq7ei8w2CQ.

14 Syed, M. (2019) *Rebel ideas: the power of diverse thinking*. London: John Murray.

15 Although some teams have found this overly prescriptive.

16 Some colleagues, however, have also found impromptu office conversations disruptive and unsettling (with no time to prepare).

Chapter 4:
Knowledge management 2.0 – after the perfect storm, sailing with AI to new discoveries

By Joe Cohen, UKIME head of innovation, and Andrea Miskolczi, Europe director of innovation, Dentons

A perfect storm?

In the last couple of years, with the hype around LegalTech and legal innovation, knowledge management became a somewhat neglected area in most law firms. Considered a static area where return on investment was difficult to prove, knowledge management had to stay in the shadows of legal innovation and LegalTech – or rebrand itself and add new focus. For many years, technological advancements targeted rather the automation and redesign of documents and processes. We seldomly saw new announcements concerning content creation and curation, or submission and search in knowledge databases.

However, with the advancement of machine learning, search, and natural language processing (NLP) technologies, advanced knowledge management teams have recently recognized the potential to utilize technology for harnessing knowhow. These teams have recognized the power of data and data mining from legal documents as a new superpower for law firms. A silent revolution around AI-assisted knowledge management has begun.

For most law firms, when the pandemic hit, knowledge management suddenly found itself in the spotlight. With the sudden shift to remote work, many lawyers had to rely on their knowledge management teams when searching for templates, best practices, or other useful materials. The lack of human touch within remote work created fewer opportunities to pop by and ask a colleague for advice or share a challenge with them in the coffee room. From the solitude of their living rooms, knowledge management databases and experienced knowledge lawyers became best friends of trainees and partners.

Technological developments, enhanced demand, and the transformation of how to access knowledge are vital components that make up the perfect storm that has been brewing within knowledge management for years. Add the pressure of increasing efficiency due to the economic recession and you get the perfect recipe for Knowledge Management 2.0 – a renewed area truly enabled by artificial intelligence (AI).

Keeping the good

Although Knowledge Management 2.0 is on the horizon, a couple of principles from the "old practice" remain very relevant. First, while it may sound trivial, we would still emphasize the core purpose of legal knowledge management – a better knowledge system for lawyers will allow them to spend less time on research, reduce risk, and increase the quality of their deliverables. In other words, it will increase efficiency – a desired outcome of countless innovation and LegalTech projects at law firms. Keeping that core purpose as your North Star helps you to prioritize efforts, succeed with change management, and demonstrate impact.

At knowledge management conferences we often hear the term "garbage in, garbage out". The principle of quality content also remains important and technology can play an important role to ensure it (as discussed below), particularly in the highly risk-oriented legal industry. Quality of content is a decisive factor to build or damage trust in the knowledge system, and trust is a fundament to the successful usage of knowledge systems – if it is gone, not even technology can easily rebuild it. Therefore, when designing your knowledge strategy, quality assurance will have to remain one of your fundamentals.

Another key principle of knowledge management is the question of culture, particularly the culture of sharing knowhow, which can really be a hidden superpower of law firms and the secret engine behind a successful, sustainable, efficient legal business. The topic of how AI can substantially improve the process of submitting content to a knowledge database will be further discussed below. However, if the culture does not support sharing such content, technology will not be able to fill the gap and make miracles "alone". The ability to share knowhow can be enhanced by technology, but the willingness remains a 100 percent human element.

Lastly, let us turn our attention to a core enabler of any good knowledge management system – humans. Technology can and will enhance knowledge management, but it cannot do it without the expertise of experienced knowledge lawyers (or practice support lawyers, as they are called in some firms). Similarly to several other areas, AI will be here to help, but not to replace humans. It removes the burden of manual tasks such as tagging content and embraces the true potential of knowledge lawyers to connect the dots, proactively build the knowledge system, and become even greater advocates for knowledge management.

Embracing the new

So, actually, what is out there in terms of technological developments for knowledge management? In this chapter, we will explore the different types of assistance that lawyers can increasingly expect from their AI-enhanced knowledge management systems.

Technologies addressing knowledge *submission*

One of the most important elements of a successful knowledge system is getting lawyers to submit their own knowledge frequently. Of course, this can take many forms – example documents, journals, advice notes, presentations and more. Unfortunately, and particularly if the lawyers in question are approaching knowledge sharing from a standing start, the *change* in mindset required to submit their own material frequently is also the hardest part.

Generally speaking, in order to submit knowledge into a system, it should be tagged so that it can later be filtered by users whilst searching. This tagging is more important in a knowledge system than, say, in a legal document management system. Here, things are organized by matters, and so whilst they may be cluttered, you usually know what you are looking for and where to find it. In a knowledge system, you're never really exactly sure what you're after – you may know the broad theme, but nothing as specific as a matter number equivalent. Therefore, the tagging system should be well developed – the accepted wisdom in many law firms is to stick to a three-tier tagging taxonomy (e.g., Employment > Contracts > Restrictive Covenants), which is replicated across all practice groups.

So, imagine you're a lawyer who has decided to submit (or, perhaps, been chased by management to do so!) their latest contract as a great example of a well-negotiated liability clause in a commercial agreement. Firstly, you need to make this process as simple as possible – ideally being able to right-click from its current location and a clear "submit to knowledge bank" button appears. Once it does so, you are now faced with a list of tags from which to select. If the list is too long, or will take up too much effort to digest, you may well give up. This is where technology can help – by analysing previously submitted documents, *it is now possible for the AI to learn and suggest the right tags for you*, therefore not only saving the lawyer time but reducing the barriers to them submitting something else in future. This is true not only for legal tags but geographical ones, knowledge types, and even document types.

Another, separate, barrier to submission is whether the document you want to submit is actually appropriate in terms of client confidentiality.

There will be some documents that are too confidential (at least for that moment in time) – usually they will live behind their own matter access walls as well.

It is possible to simply stop there and say that we will not ask our lawyers to submit anything that has enhanced security permissions. However, in doing so you may be missing a trick, as it is precisely this material that can embody the latest knowledge. One way to get around this is via (automated) redaction – i.e., at the submission stage, asking the machine to redact any mentions of company or individual names, logos, quantities, prices etc. Done in the right way, this could allow the submission of lots of extra knowledge without risking any internal disclosure of data that is meant to be hidden. However, there will be some documents that are too confidential to share in a knowledge system even after redaction.

The final element of making knowledge submission easier looks at something at the highest level of abstraction – what is good knowledge? Because this can take some thought, effort, and time from the fee earner, inevitably it leads to less knowledge being submitted than there is available throughout the firm. Therefore, if a system can pre-identify, or at least recommend, potential suitable knowledge for submission, that would be incredibly useful.

It is not necessarily easy to pinpoint how this would be done, however interesting factors that could be explored include:

- How frequently certain documents are accessed after matters are closed by different people;
- How many times specific PLC articles are searched for; or
- How frequently people's individual profiles are searched for in the knowledge system.

This would come under the category of efficient and useful knowledge data mining.

Technologies addressing knowledge *searching*

If the previous section was considering how to enable easier knowledge submission, the logical next step is to explore how to make the actual searching experience of such a system as easy and straightforward as possible for the lawyer.

We've already spoken about the importance of having good filters, and it is similarly important to have a good search bar. In this way, lawyers should be able to find something useful to them quite quickly. Taking a step further, having a "see more like this" or an "other people viewed this" feature adds crowdsourcing and machine learning elements that should definitely be considered. This goes for not only knowledge content but also knowledge contributors – that is to say, a "see similar contributors" feature.

Looking deeper into the machine learning possibilities, we will now borrow something from the legal due diligence world and introduce data extraction into the mix. The ability of algorithms to extract clauses and classify entire documents will remove the need for the lawyers or system admins to do it, and make our filtering experience a lot richer. It also brings up the possibility of scanning some subsets of our document system to look for specific data points that might be useful to the deal you're working on. Wouldn't it be nice, when you are working on a document and are confronted by a particularly tricky clause that you've not worked on before, to set the AI looking for similar clauses to help your drafting? It is precisely these efficiencies that not only save lawyer time in researching, but also help to surface things that would otherwise have not been found, and therefore increase quality.

For those that have used similar AI or machine learning software, you may be thinking – what if the machine makes a mistake and either misses a clause or miscategorizes it? To answer this question, we need to think about our expectations in each scenario. In the case of due diligence, the bar is very high – if we are relying on the machine to extract large numbers of clauses correctly and it misses some of them, that could have serious consequences for the law firm. It is for this reason that lawyers tend not to rely on the AI outputs at the moment and still do further exploration. Using the same extraction technology for knowledge has a lower bar, however, as if certain clauses are missed you are no worse off than you were beforehand without the system.

Beyond the old

As mentioned above, the core purpose of knowledge management is to increase efficiency and enable lawyers to deliver their legal advisory services faster and cheaper. Furthermore, Knowledge Management 2.0 provides an opportunity beyond that – tapping into the law firm's legal knowledge beyond current limits and harnessing the information that "we don't know we have". Legal trends, best practices for drafting certain clauses and managing cases, and regulatory bodies' focusing on their supervisory activities are just a few examples from the many that we will be able to discover by mining and analyzing legal documents and other types of legal data.

The pioneering law firms already collect and analyze such data with the help of AI to create business value out of it for themselves and for their clients. The more data such firms have, and are able to access, the more insight and value can be created. So, for this opportunity, size does matter. But, as with so many things connected to AI, the entire industry – whether small firms or large ones – is just at the very beginning of an exponential journey…

The views, thoughts, and opinions expressed in this chapter belong solely to the authors, and not necessarily to the authors' employer.

Chapter 5:
Data-driven knowledge-based management

By Jonna Vainikainen, business process manager, Castrén & Snellman Attorneys Ltd

Contrary to popular belief, data is not synonymous with information. Data is – or at least should be – a fact or a collection of facts, while information puts these facts into context. While data is raw and unorganized, information is organized. Units of information, or data points, are discrete and sometimes unrelated. Information maps out these data points to provide a big-picture view of how it all fits together. In this chapter, I will discuss the role of data in law firms and the transition from knowledge management to data-driven knowledge-based management that is currently ongoing in the legal sector.

The evolving role of knowledge management

Traditionally, knowledge management departments retrieve and forward data. This data can be, for example, data from official documents, such as trade register extracts. Drawing a line between data and information is not always easy. Are trade register extracts or financial statements already information or just a collection of data? Regardless of the answer, knowledge management (KM) usually has access to an extensive legal library, electronic literature, and numerous legal and corporate databases. Using carefully selected sources, KM departments compile the most significant news and legislative amendments, essential material by the authorities, relevant case law, and most recent legal literature into concise packages for their client.

Many KM departments help clients keep up to date with the latest regulatory changes affecting their business. Information services specialize in researching and retrieving relevant information for various fields of law, monitoring legislative reforms and case law, and drafting memoranda and newsletters tailored to specific needs. If a client needs to follow the news and developments relating to a specific business sector or field of law, the KM department can monitor these for them. This can be done in a comprehensive and cost-efficient manner, but only if the data is of high quality.

Although raw data is rarely used in traditional knowledge management as such, data processing is an inherent part of KM work. Data processing can include, for example, retrieving information from a national register or statistics office and modifying it to be in a more understandable format. It can also include using data to find an answer for a specific question. Software robots can also be used in the retrieval of official documents. Through API (Application Programming Interface) integrations, these robots can use the data in different ways and make it easier for KM departments to process the data further.

Data quality – good enough and fit for purpose

There is no use in processing data that is of poor quality. But how can we determine whether the quality of a specific dataset is good or poor? Does good-quality data mean that the data itself is of high quality according to data quality rules, or that the data can be used and exploited according to certain specifications or defined targets?

In my opinion, the data itself can be of good quality, but if it cannot be used as intended it is still useless. When assessing the quality of data, we can apply the steps we already know from process improvement. We start by defining the needs and expectations of the data management clients and the interest groups. Second, we define the strategies, the goals, and the services to be provided as well as the data needed for the delivery of the services. In the implementation phase, we act as planned. Once everything is done, we collect the data and check if we have reached the strategies and goals defined earlier. If not, changes need to be made. If yes, we can still probably find something to improve.

Mistakes can happen in knowledge management work if:

- Data is missing and therefore the work cannot be performed;
- Information is unclear and therefore the work cannot be done without further clarification;
- The data is of poor quality and therefore the work (e.g., indexing in legal tech projects) cannot be done or is done incorrectly; or
- The people and teams do not follow the planned process.[1]

Mistakes can result in the client rejecting the outcome as faulty and requiring the work to be redone, causing additional expenses and a delay in delivery.

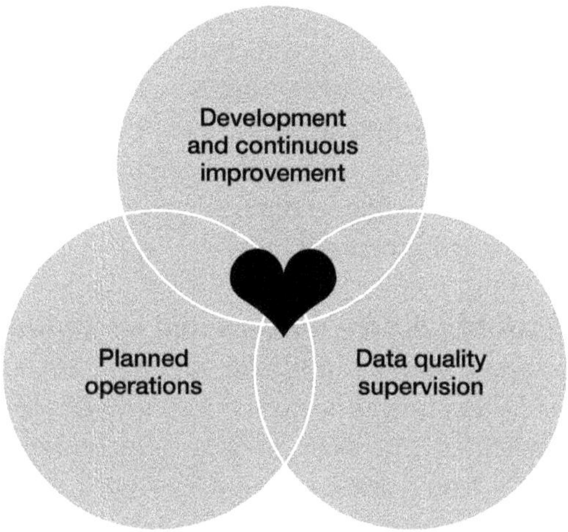

Figure 1: The heart of success lies in the intersection of systematic data quality supervision, operations that run as planned, and development whenever needed.

The importance of good-quality data

It is advisable to measure the quality of data to keep it "fit" and to keep it available to relevant people. However, data does not need to be perfect or faultless. It needs to be good enough to allow for good business decisions, which means that it needs to be good enough to reduce mistakes in and uncertainty of decisions.

The business of law is a business of trust, and, for better or for worse, data quality affects client relationships. It is impossible to use poor-quality data in knowledge management work, especially since KM departments mainly reprocess data that is already in a processed form. It is therefore paramount how and in what form the data is provided. Data that is primarily of good quality makes knowledge management work more reliable.

Good-quality data is a competitive advantage. It enables effective time management as users do not need to spend time correcting or modifying the data. In the legal industry, where value is typically based on hours used, it is the client who ultimately benefits from the effective management of time.

Good-quality data also comes in handy when automation and reporting tools are being built. If the data is of poor quality, many exceptions need to be managed in the development phase. This is time-consuming, more expensive, and makes the change process more difficult to handle. If mistakes are found in a later phase, it will take much more time to fix them. If data cannot be used because the quality is weak, it is easily forgotten. In the world of business intelligence, poor-quality data can sometimes result in an unwillingness to use the data, which in turn leads to an unwillingness to improve data quality. Sometimes the best option is to make poor-quality data visible by reporting it or by other means, and in that way encourage improvement.

Ensuring good-quality data – metrics and evaluation

Typically, mistakes will make a task take ten to 30 times longer than it otherwise would.[2] When mistakes are reduced and the degree of success is subsequently increased, the same number of employees can get more work done and, as a result, increase productivity. It is therefore important to evaluate and measure the quality of data and to define metrics to ensure that the data meets the required standards. Metrics refers to numeric, quantifiable meters for evaluating outcomes and performance, and for creating forecasts based on earlier data.

Good-quality data combined with carefully selected metrics yields many benefits. It helps in forecasting the future and provides information to support decisions. In executing strategy, it can be used for communicating important goals, converting company strategy to achievable goals and tasks, and monitoring strategy implementation. In personnel management, the combination is a very useful tool for steering employee activity and for motivating, supporting, acknowledging, and rewarding performance. At operational level, it can provide insight into learning and analysing, measuring the current level of operations, finding mistakes or problems, increasing the probability of success, and measuring delivery cycles both internally and with clients. It can also be used to create more accurate offers and strategic, measurable goals.

When measuring data, it is possible to examine the past, the present, and the future. Information from the past is something that many companies have been analysing for years using various reporting tools. Nowadays it is increasingly common to use metrics to predict the future.

Typically, metrics are used to measure the current status of a specific function (maintenance metrics) or the success of a specific change management initiative (change metrics). When evaluating maintenance, the basic task can be defined by the organization itself or given by an external organization. Self-defined tasks typically relate to measuring things like working time, costs, offers won and lost, the sales pipeline, and productivity. Externally given tasks can relate, for example, to requirements imposed by legislation, such as MAR (Market Abuse Regulation), the

GDPR, sanctions, and KYC (Know Your Client) regulations. Given tasks can also be introduced by a client or an interest group, e.g., by another law firm or a network of law firms. Change tasks relate to future expectations, strategic measurement, and metrics that measure change itself.

When evaluating the quality of data, metrics need to meet some essential requirements. As stated above, data needs to fit specific needs, otherwise it is useless. Good requirements for the metrics are:

- *Relevance.* The meter needs to be relevant for the decision-maker. Relevance can depend either on the data or the situation;
- *Economic efficiency.* The meter needs to be economical. Creating a meter should not take up too many resources when compared to its relevance;
- *Validity.* The meter needs to be able to evaluate the defined purpose;
- *Reliability.* The meter needs to be accurate enough and outcomes cannot vary too much;
- *Credibility.* The meter needs to be credible so that decision-makers can rely on it when making decisions;
- *Monitorability.* The meter needs to be easy to monitor. If it is too labour-consuming, it is too easy to neglect; and
- *Sensitivity.* The meter needs to be sensitive to changes and easy and quick to change.

The rising era of data-driven technologies and automatization

Technology has made a major breakthrough in the legal industry in the past decade. This knowledge-intensive profession is seeing rapid change from time-consuming work to technology-assisted work. Figure 2 overleaf presents the implementation of technology from the lawyers' perspective.

Lawyers spend at least 20 percent of their time drafting or editing documents	Technologies should be functional and a natural part of the work	Organization culture steers the implementation of new technologies	In their role, lawyers are constantly under pressure and there is little time to learn new technologies
How to reward faster development of know-how in lawyers' careers?	Technology benefits: decrease of manual work, sensibility of work	Tailor-made software for law firms or developing own technologies?	Piloting and agile development

Figure 2: Technology implementation through the eyes of a lawyer.

Data processing and calculation rules need to be clearly defined in line with business needs to ensure good-quality reporting and forecasting. Data warehouses can be used to help meet these needs by automating data flows and by combining data from different sources. This will free up resources as time can be spent on analysing the data instead of collecting it. Below are some examples of time-saving technologies that can be of assistance in the legal world.

Software robots

Software robots can assist in harnessing raw data for knowledge management. Robots can collect data from several sources and collate it for further processing. They can also retrieve specific information, e.g., trade register extracts and other relevant documents, and save it to a pre-defined location. Robots can work at least five times faster than humans and rarely make mistakes (when robots do make mistakes, it is mainly because humans have taught them wrongly), so they are major time-savers. Law firms also use software robots for mandatory administrative tasks such as conflict of interest checks, sanction checks, and know-your-client processes. These regulated checks have significantly increased administrative work in law firms. In some firms, these tasks fall to the KM department, but many law firms have their own risk management departments with dedicated personnel to do this work on a daily basis.

Software robots can bring many fast benefits, save time, and increase work satisfaction by reducing manual labor. Long working days are not an obstacle for software robots. They do their work as they are trained and do not think for themselves – for better or for worse. Automation not only improves efficiency, but also minimizes the risk of human error.

Automated documents

When drafting documents, lawyers can spend hours modifying old templates and writing new contracts from scratch. Automated contract-drafting takes care of these steps, allowing lawyers to spend more time on analytical tasks.

Data can be used to automate documents that can be used by law firms themselves or offered to clients. Automated documents save time as you simply fill in the information on the correct data fields in a form and then download the finished document for your use. The document layout is always correct, and the content is up to date. A good document automation tool speeds up the drafting of documents and is easy to use.

Other legal technologies

There are many technologies in the market that rapidly read, analyze, and form an understanding of documents before displaying the results of the analysis to the user in a clear format. The resulting data can be organized in different ways, previewed, and edited if necessary. Many of these technologies create automated documents, such as briefs or signing bibles. These technologies use different kinds of workflows and even artificial intelligence, such as machine learning, to automate low-level tasks, freeing up resources for strategic thinking, analysis, and advice. Machine learning involves inference, deep learning, natural language processing, and pattern recognition. Many law firms use these technologies in litigations, mergers and acquisitions, and finance.

Technologies are also developed rapidly to help with administrative work, such as the KYC and sanction checks mentioned earlier, or to alleviate manual work caused by the GDPR. The information collected from the client is decided in the implementation phase, which means that the risk-based nature of the Money Laundering Act can be accounted for and the collection of the client information is better targeted. As law firms might handle assignments with different risk profiles for an individual client, the products allow assignment-specific risk assessments so that different levels of risk can be documented on a case-by-case basis.

In addition to technologies that are tailor-made for law firms, there are technologies to support work from home:

- *Electronic signature products.* These provide basic and strong eSignatures that are fully compliant with the EU's eIDAS digital identification regulation and provide a secure, legally binding method to sign documents online.
- *Online contract management.* This allows the user to easily add and search for contracts as well as add different kinds of reminders depending on what needs to be done.
- *Authentication solutions.* These provide fast, secure identity and authentication, also for mobile devices.

With the help of these technologies, lawyers can advise their clients quickly and the law firm gains the competitive edge by doing work more effectively while reducing costs.

Legal industry trends call for good-quality data

Good-quality data supports the multitude of trends in the legal industry. Some of the most notable trends are outlined below.

Amount of data and criticism of sources

The amount of data and information is increasing, and it has become harder to handle. The significance of data and electronic information has also increased, but the accessibility is relevant. While data may appear to be from a reliable source, it is more important than ever to practice proper source criticism. In a world where anyone can publish an article through a seemingly reliable channel, the skill of source criticism is crucial. These days it is quite easy for fake information to seem reliable, and even authorities find it difficult to separate the two. The significance of being critical of sources, it seems, is not valued enough. The increasing number of data sources makes this criticism even harder. In addition, for certain professions (such as lawyers), the importance of data and information has increased.

The COVID-19 crisis and recent data breaches have highlighted the importance of trustworthy data processing. In its white paper on artificial intelligence, the European Commission emphasized that trustworthiness is a prerequisite for the adoption of digital technology, and ethical AI is one of the EU's key goals.[3] Algorithmic biases are a particular risk that can undermine the trustworthiness of AI, and everyone developing or adopting AI applications should be prepared to deal with such biases. According to the EC's Ethics Guidelines, AI should be trustworthy, lawful, and ethical, as well as robust from a technical perspective, which would not be possible without quality data.

Technologies and legal tech

Technologies have become more important as a result of the rapid increase in the amount of data. Technologies are used to make data and information handling more effective than before. However, law firms do not make use of the different technologies as much and as well as they could and should. It must be admitted that it is hard to keep up with the pace of all technical developments. In addition, there are many legacy systems in law firms that can sometimes be very hard to abandon. Law firms have made huge investments in different technologies during recent years and do have the resources to do so. The challenge is that often firms do not end up gaining the potential output capacity of the technologies they invested in. It is not a question of the technology's potential – the potential is eroded away by company culture. Established practices are slowing down and, in the worst case, preventing the adaptation of new technologies.

Legal technology is a red-hot market where new solutions are constantly emerging, putting pressure on law firms to make use of them. Since legal tasks have traditionally included routine tasks and static working methods, many believe that early adopters of legal technology will have a significant edge over their competitors. However, the media often oversimplifies the implementation process of legal technology, giving the impression that innovative IT-based solutions immediately eliminate routine tasks and even replace legal expertise. Big consulting and auditing firms are entering the law firm market and are eager to disrupt the traditional legal services model with their data-driven solutions that are based on their data analytics and data processing capabilities. As mentioned earlier, the data needs to be of high quality in order to make these solutions useful and cost-effective.

Legal design

Legal design is a user-centric approach for creating better legal products and services for our clients. Visualizing legal content and services is one way to make them more understandable and often more attractive. For example, designed contracts are easier to understand and less likely to be misinterpreted as the terms of the contract are clear to the parties. Designed, clear contracts are also easier to automate than complex documentation, making the whole process of drafting contracts simpler and faster.

At their best, legal design projects are carried out in a multi-professional team consisting of linguists, graphic designers, lawyers, and IT and legal technology experts. Typically, the client also plays an active role throughout the design process and the project is wrapped up in a feedback session that benefits all parties involved. With legal design, we can make the law more understandable and user-centric together.

Sustainability

Sustainability-related regulation is likely to increase, and companies need to make sure that sustainability data is up to date and of good quality. One regulatory initiative is the European Union's proposed Corporate Sustainability Reporting Directive,[4] which broadens the scope of the Non-Financial Reporting Directive. One of the goals of the proposal is to make sustainability information as standardized and reliable as financial information. The proposal anticipates the increasing digitalization of sustainability information by requiring that the reported information should be in a digitalized format so that is easier to compare across firms. It is not just client companies who must meet the new standards in sustainability data – the Corporate Sustainability Reporting Directive would concern a number of large law firms that are currently not obligated to report non-financial information. If data is not of good quality, it is impossible to do the abovementioned comparison.

Conclusion

The legal industry is undergoing a rapid change where a wide range of conceptual and technological innovations and approaches are being incorporated into lawyers' daily lives. Be it data mining, document automation, or business intelligence, today's lawyers need to process more information than ever before. In addition, continuously increasing regulation puts pressure on the efficient processing of information and data. All these trends call for good-quality data across the whole organization. We are now seeing a change in the legal industry whereby knowledge management is not merely a separate function of a law firm but increasingly a mindset that lays the foundation for knowledge-based management that guides the work of every employee.

References

1 Adapted from Torkkola, S. (2017), Lean asiantuntijatyön johtamisessa, Alma Talent, pp. 185-198. Translation by the author.

2 Torkkola, S. (2017), Lean asiantuntijatyön johtamisessa, Alma Talent, pp. 185-198.

3 https://digital-strategy.ec.europa.eu/en/library/ethics-guidelines-trustworthy-ai

4 https://ec.europa.eu/commission/presscorner/detail/en/qanda_21_1806

Chapter 6:
Legal technology and knowledge management

By Elisabeth Cappuyns, director of knowledge management, DLA Piper LLP (US)

Context

As we have all experienced in our daily lives, technology can reduce mundane and repetitive tasks and generally make our lives easier. Similarly, legal technology can add value by helping attorneys produce higher quality work more efficiently, consistently, and accountably, plus it can improve attorneys' quality of life by reducing time-consuming and onerous manual, routine, and administrative tasks in their workflows. Technology tools have been available in the business and professional world for many years, but they have matured and proliferated in the legal industry significantly since the mid-2010s and they are now part of the evolving practice of law. Even so, while some in-house legal departments were starting to adopt certain targeted technology solutions, most large law firms did not make it a priority to adopt a wide range of legal technology tools beyond their foundational technology offerings until recently. This was likely due to the significant budgets and people necessary to implement the tools properly, and because the legal profession is typically more comfortable maintaining its existing approaches and more reluctant to embrace technology in its daily workflows.

Then the world changed in March 2020, when the COVID-19 pandemic forced most professions, including the legal profession, to quickly adapt to a number of major changes. These changes included the need for most legal professionals to abruptly start working from home and change the way they performed their work, thereby meaningfully altering the legal industry. After the initial rush to set up people to work remotely with access to computers and communication tools, for what was at first expected to be a short period of time, it became clear that the pandemic and its effects would last much longer and that many attorneys would continue to work remotely at least part of the time. Soon, law firms and legal departments realized the role of technology as a valuable resource to support the changing demands of the legal workforce and to optimize attorneys' time, and they became more open to adopting additional technology tools.

Developing trends

As a result of the preceding context, both attorneys and their clients (in-house counsel and business contacts) now expect the use of relevant legal technology tools as part of the legal service offering, to streamline processes, and make them more efficient and consistent. This is true for both junior attorneys, who often prefer to use technology and work collaboratively using these tools, and more senior attorneys, who have billing and client relationship responsibilities and want to improve the value and efficiencies of their legal services. Investment in technology can also help with recruiting and retention efforts, as attorneys want to work smarter, not harder, to accomplish their work. As clients' emphasis is focused less on the billable hour and more on relationships and outcomes, they expect their attorneys to use state-of-the-art technology and tools to perform their legal work. The use of technology has become table stakes, as the practice of law is changing to encompass the additional functionality and resources technology offers, as an essential, even if often invisible, component of contemporary law practice. In-house counsel in particular, responsible for their organization's legal budgets, expect more from their external counsel than merely delivering excellent legal work. The use of technology also allows law firms to provide value-adds to their clients, including extranets and KM consulting, and the potential for direct collaborations with clients, which clients have come to expect and appreciate.

This interest in legal technology tools is also evident in both the formation of numerous start-up technology companies offering new legal solutions, and in the large financial investments in legal technology in the last few years, especially in 2021,[1] with a decrease so far in 2022.[2] During that time, several legal technology companies have gone public, achieved unicorn status, and are getting funded at large valuations.[3] In addition, the larger technology players in the industry are acquiring other legal technology companies, both big and small. As a result, we are seeing both a consolidation of some of the more established tools, often with mixed results for the products themselves, and a continuing diversity of new players and solutions in the legal technology market. Some of the main reasons for the financial investments in these tools are increasing client expectations, the increased maturity and sophistication of many legal technology tools, plus their more targeted applications, and the belief that the typical slower adoption in the legal industry means more potential for growth.

The current legal technology landscape and the growing expectations of attorneys and clients in turn provide an opportunity for KM teams to help identify, test, and implement the most useful tools for their organizations. While certain technology tools have been around for a long time and have become commonplace in the legal industry (such as e-discovery tools, intranets, and databases), in the last few years other types of tools have become more tailored and customized for a legal audience, making them more useful in the legal industry (such as artificial intelligence (AI)-based document review and drafting tools, and data analytics). KM teams can manage and assist in the application of relevant and targeted technology tools to support various legal practices. In addition, more law firms started to move to the cloud even before the pandemic, which requires technology that supports these migrations and platforms, plus trained IT professionals to implement the changes.

Overview of legal technology tools

The most common legal technology tools, organized in broad categories, include the following:

- AI-based document review and drafting;
- Blockchain;
- Communication and collaboration platforms;
- Data analytics and data projects;
- Databases;
- Document automation;
- E-discovery;
- Electronic signatures;
- Enterprise and targeted search;
- Intranets and extranets;
- Low/no-code tools;
- Matter profiling and experience management;
- Operational tools, such as electronic billing;
- Robotic process automation (RPA); and
- Workflow process and matter management tools.

With the onset of the pandemic, attorneys needed practical legal technology tools focused on their daily practice of law to advise their clients that would support their new work circumstances. The most useful tools let users collaborate virtually by improving their processes, which allows them to benefit from both internal and external data, and each other's expertise and relevant work product remotely, as people are often not in the office to ask for help. In addition, client expectations about incorporating technology to streamline work product and make it more efficient, plus improvements in certain tools, became an opportunity for KM teams to showcase and implement the functionality of those tools.

Here are a few examples to show how the use of legal technology tools has developed recently.

Communication and collaboration platforms

During the pandemic, communication and collaboration tools were one of the first types of technology tools to take hold in attorneys' and other professionals' everyday life. Some tools like Zoom are focused on video conferencing, with related functionality such as sharing screens, chats, Q&A, polls, and break-out rooms. This allows remote teams to work together on documents and strategy sessions, as they would have done in live settings, and it is also used in depositions and court proceedings. In addition to this typical communication functionality, tools like Teams also allow teams to share and organize documents and collaborate on them in real-time. While the document management functionality is limited and requires careful processes for version control and access rights, it has been helpful to be able to approximate some in-person collaboration.

Data analytics and data projects

As the world becomes more data-centric and data-driven, the legal industry has similarly become more interested in using and optimizing the available data in legal practice. This data can include both publicly-available data, such as information relating to court cases and regulatory filings, and internal data, unique to the organization and its clients. The easiest of these sources to obtain are publicly-available data, and several data analytics tools – such as Lex Machina and Deal Point Data – are available and expanding their scope. These tools capture and analyze data on issues ranging from the typical time to get court and regulatory decisions and the likelihood of the outcome, to details about an individual judge's track record on certain types of motions, to typical deal terms in certain types of transactions. These data points can help teams strategize about their matters and advise their clients on likely outcomes, especially when attorneys and law firms add their own experience to the mix. Data projects that combine public and private data and expertise are very popular in legal organizations, and legal technology vendors are increasingly willing and able to provide APIs (application programming interfaces) to facilitate the integration of platforms and large amounts of data between systems to support these efforts. Once the data has been identified and analyzed, it is helpful to use data visualizations to make it easier for the audience to understand the results.

Document automation

Document automation tools allow the user to create an initial draft of a document (or suite of related documents) by using software to identify and complete variable fields in the relevant locations in an agreed upon form (or suite of forms) by completing a questionnaire with the relevant information, such as the deal terms in a transaction. The tool can also include conditional provisions that are triggered (or not) by the responses in the questionnaire, thereby allowing for a large range of different options in one form. These tools, such as Contract Express and HotDocs, require coding on the back-end to prepare and tag the form(s) correctly to ingest the relevant information in the right locations. A related tool is the clause bank, which allows the user to collect and organize best in class or favorite clauses for certain types of documents, so they can easily be inserted into the document being drafted. Ideally, the clause bank is integrated in the document management system to make it easier to insert and format the clause directly into the document. The benefit of these tools is that once attorneys have agreed upon a form for a certain type of matter or client, the upfront coding work can be worthwhile to streamline the initial drafting process by making it faster and more consistent, while allowing for a range of options to be selected upfront. This became very helpful and popular when attorneys were no longer able to confer in the office and instead needed to be able to easily identify the relevant starting points for their draft documents.

Matter profiling and experience management

One of the more useful and obvious ways to optimize the work of attorneys is to refer to and build on their prior work experience, both as individuals and as a firm. There are technology tools, such as Intapp's Experience and (now) Litera's Foundation, that help an organization profile its matters and collect details about its prior experience, which is then searchable to identify relevant information. This information can be used for pricing and budgeting estimates, to find attorneys with relevant experience in certain practice areas or "experts" on specific issues, and to identity trends in certain types of matters. The main obstacle for these tools is that they typically require a significant amount of input from the attorneys working on the matters to collect as much useful information as possible, which is usually challenging to obtain.

Workflow process and matter management

Workflow process and matter management tools typically streamline and improve repetitive processes to make them more efficient and the parties involved more accountable. Many types of tools fit in this broad category, ranging from general project management and contract lifecycle management tools to case management platforms and deal management tools. As these tools make it easier for a team to identify and connect members, coordinate and assign tasks, track statuses and updates, and organize digital assets, including electronic signatures, they became even more important and relevant during the pandemic, when teams were working remotely. As the hybrid work environment continues, these tools will support further expanding use cases and far-flung teams.

AI tools

A continuing trend in the legal industry since a few years before the pandemic is the use of various AI-based tools with a range of machine learning approaches, including deep learning and neural networks, such as Kira, eBrevia, Luminence, and Casetext/Compose. Many of these tools allow users to process and review documents for certain provisions and terms more quickly, plus you can teach the tool to identify new provisions. In addition, these tools can help prepare initial draft court filings using established standards and case law references, and more recently, AI tools are being used to help predict legal outcomes in a range of matters. While these AI-based tools have meaningfully matured in the last few years and have generally become accepted as a reliable technology, there is often still a disconnect between most attorneys' expectations of what an AI-based tool can and should do and what it actually can do with and without extensive training protocols. The marketing hype can sometimes result in disappointment, so KM teams need to help manage expectations and move the legal industry to a more realistic place for this use of legal technology. In addition, there are many efforts to understand and guide the ethical and legal implications of using AI tools in legal matters, resulting in developing rules and regulations across jurisdictions. For a more in-depth and technical review of AI, see chapter seven.

Some of these tools can be used in both disputes and transactional practices, such as collaboration and experience management tools, but others have been customized for certain types of practices, such as deal management tools for transactional practices. In addition, most of these tools can be used by attorneys in law firms or in in-house legal departments, but some are more typically used in one organization than another. This often depends on the specific needs of the attorneys, plus the cost-effectiveness of acquiring a tool based on the range of applications and scale of usage. For example, contract lifecycle management tools are more typically used in legal departments and matter management tools in law firms.

To find out more information about the types of available legal technology tools and their specific functionality, you can check one of several recently launched legal technology directories, including LawNext legal tech directory,[4] Legaltech Hub,[5] Legal IT Professionals legal tech directory,[6] and CLOC's new LegalTech platform and vendor directory.[7]

Additional considerations

Within law firms, the increased use and application of technology has been both championed and supported by KM teams. KM teams can help to identify, pilot, launch, and help with adoption of new technology, so the changed work environment during the pandemic allowed KM teams to demonstrate how the right legal technology tools could support the attorneys' practices beyond the remote work environment to improve their work experience generally. A KM team's knowledge of the legal technology market and the quality and functionality of the available solutions is an important part of the assessment of any new investment in or replacement of current tools. In addition, before the end users (the attorneys) even see a new technology tool, KM professionals can help guide a project through a proof of concept or pilot process to see how it works, if it works as expected, and if it is practical enough to use and implement, so any issues are identified quickly and either fixed or the project is finished. KM teams typically include attorneys who are liaisons to help bridge any gaps between the technology teams and the attorneys, and who add their legal subject matter expertise and experiences to the application of the tool to optimize it and encourage adoption, because the more attorneys use the tools, the more helpful they tend to be.

Therefore, it is important for KM to be involved and consulted in an organization's decisions about next generation technology tools. Some important considerations when assessing new technology include the following:

- Does the proposed technology support the organization's business strategy and goals?
- Do you already have technology that can perform the necessary function?
- If not, does the new technology integrate and connect easily with your existing systems?
- Have you compared different vendors and is the vendor reputable and collaborative?
- Is the UI/UX easy to use?
- What are the tool's capabilities for reporting and metrics?

Even though during and since the pandemic, attorneys (and clients) were more willing to try and adopt the tools they needed to continue their work, there have also been some drawbacks and additional considerations. In particular, the rapid shift to remote work and the steep increase in the use of technology tools and their related learning curves resulted in a certain tech fatigue. This has created adoption challenges beyond the typical change management issues that arise when introducing a new tool or approach to the way people work, and the KM and IT teams implementing new tools have to carefully assess when to roll out which tools and how to optimize the best adoption, for example by staggering rollout schedules and offering a range of training options. In addition, as more attorneys are using more tools more frequently and becoming more sophisticated users, there is less of a concern about losing legal jobs to robots (or technology), but also a higher expectation of the availability of relevant and functioning technology tools, with resulting frustrations when the tools do not work properly or perform as expected.

In addition, while law firms have been more willing to consider and purchase new technology to support the changing work environment and prepare themselves for the evolving practice of law, this has resulted in higher ongoing operational technology costs and budget pressures. The higher costs are caused by a range of factors, including the increase in technology investments, such as investments in protections against cyber-attacks and data breaches, most technology tools becoming more expensive, and the ongoing, but challenging, trend of migration to the cloud for foundational technology platforms. The move towards a hybrid work model also requires technology investments on multiple fronts, including upgrading office audio and video equipment and supporting home offices, although some of this will likely be offset over time by a reduction in real estate costs as office footprints are shrinking. At the same time, because many law firms have already made significant investments in technology in the last few years, resulting in fewer immediate needs for new solutions, and as organizations are preparing for a possible economic downturn, we may see a continuation of the decrease in legal technology funding so far in 2022. Another way to satisfy the need for useful technology tools has been to increase adoption of existing technology tools and to expand the use cases and functionality of the existing technology tools to solve demands where possible.

There are also other approaches to the use of legal technology tools outside of the law firm environment. In-house and legal operations departments have made strides in implementing the tools most relevant to their workflows, often triggered by budget constraints and supported by the Corporate Legal Operations Consortium, and in some cases in collaboration with law firm partners and/or vendors to increase the functionality of certain tools. This allows legal departments to streamline their workflows and results and gives law firms an opportunity to solidify and deepen relationships with their clients. In addition, ALSPs, or alternative legal service providers, have typically embraced the use of technology to allow them to be more competitive in their pricing by streamlining and automating their workflows. Some law firms have formed separate subsidiaries to create their own technology solutions, support their client relationships, or make investments in other legal technology.

Conclusion

As a fitting end to this chapter, it is important to note that attorneys have an obligation of technical competence, or the obligation to understand the technology used in the practice of law, as part of their responsibility to their clients. The American Bar Association's (ABA) Model Rule 1.1 comments already required attorneys to stay up to date on changes in the law and its practice, but in 2012, the ABA officially added Comment 8 to the Model Rule of Professional Conduct 1.1. This comment states:

> *"To maintain the requisite knowledge and skill, a lawyer should keep abreast of changes in the law and its practice, including the benefits and risks associated with relevant technology, engage in continuing study and education and comply with all continuing legal education requirements to which the lawyer is subject."*[8]

As a result, attorneys cannot claim that they are not "computer literate" or "tech savvy", as ignorance or unfamiliarity with technology is no longer an excuse to avoid their obligation to be knowledgeable about software and hardware. As of mid-2022, 40 states had adopted this revised language into their Rules of Professional Conduct.[9] Related to this development, it will be interesting to see if and how more law schools will incorporate the use and understanding of legal technology tools into their curricula.

Clearly, the role of legal technology and related KM efforts has been solidified and has expanded since the pandemic, and we now have the opportunity to identify and implement the best next steps to continue to support the evolving practice of law.

References

1 www.law360.com/pulse/articles/1458718/legal-tech-smashed-investment-records-in-2021
2 www.artificiallawyer.com/2022/06/15/is-legal-tech-facing-a-vc-funding-crunch/
3 www.reuters.com/legal/transactional/legal-tech-buzzed-throughout-2021-with-ipos-new-unicorns-2021-12-29/
4 https://directory.lawnext.com
5 https://www.legaltechnologyhub.com
6 https://www.legalitprofessionals.com/legal-it-supplier-directory
7 https://ecosystem.theoremlegal.com/a/cloc
8 www.americanbar.org/groups/professional_responsibility/publications/model_rules_of_professional_conduct/rule_1_1_competence/comment_on_rule_1_1/
9 www.lawnext.com/tech-competence

Chapter 7: Artificial intelligence and automation

By James Loft, COO, Rainbird Technologies

Artificial intelligence and automation in knowledge-driven industries

Artificial intelligence and automation have for some time been considered too simplistic to handle the complexity and scale required for knowledge-intensive organizations and are often shelved when it comes to strategic organizational planning.

Despite the advent of Intelligent Automation, the result of a combination of artificial intelligence, Robotic Process Automation, and Business Process Management (BPM), the belief still remains that automation is for simple activities and artificial intelligence is a data-hungry black box that is unreachable for most.

The hype surrounding chatbots, self-driving cars, and AlphaGo machines has taken the focus away from "enterprise-ready" sets of tools that many in the technology field have been working on for some time. These tools, if given the appropriate time and resources, are capable of opening doors of possibility that previously remained closed to organizations keen to automate and augment their operations.

In order to best discuss possible factors for success and the benefits of artificial intelligence, especially in the knowledge space, it is important to be explicit from the start as to what is specifically meant by AI. In the widest sense it is not a new term or theory, nor is it new in practice, as mechanical calculation machines have been in existence since the Middle Ages. Completing tasks previously undertaken by humans, systems such as ABS braking have been present in cars since their launch within the aviation industry in the late 1960s.

Process automation, which is focused on simple tasks like invoice processing or copy and paste style tasks, has been useful to knowledge-intensive industries, but not game-changing. On the other hand, artificial intelligence focuses on a data starting point and can predict the outcomes of events that would otherwise take a huge amount of human experience to foresee. AI of this type is a needy and hungry partner that requires large amounts of data and struggles to explain its reasoning. In the legal industry, that takes the form of predictive systems for contract reviews, which scan for keywords to predict the outcomes of a trial, which is then passed to a human operator to review and make a decision before an action is taken. It is therefore reasonable to assume that if your need is to codify a specialism or any kind of complexity, then the available technology is not ready to support it. However, there has been a shift over recent years toward the concept of automating human decision-making instead of just manual processes and tasks.

Unlocking automated decisioning

Automated decision-making technology has matured, and artificial intelligence technologies are beginning to emerge. Despite existing for a very long time, automated decision-making enterprises sit within the gray area between the two examples above, and often focus on using a mixture of data sources and codified human expertise. These systems are still based on rules but are supercharged by artificial intelligence.

Technologies that bring this revolution are rules-based, but they are the first of their kind to add a blanket of probabilistic-based reasoning in the same way that humans do when they interpret or apply such rules. We deploy rules all the time throughout our lives and apply inference as a layer over the top. Even simple decisions such as what to have for lunch are given a light touch of probabilistic-based reasoning and inference, but as scenarios become more complex the human brain falls short when speed, accuracy, and consistency are critical.

The way to think about this is to think of knowledge as being in two tiers, the first of which is a codified set of expertise that acts as an ontology of the subject matter. More often than not, technology has been designed in this space to create a visual representation or interface so that you do not need to learn how to code, or hire a coder, to benefit.

This requirement to think in a nonlinear way and capture it visually is possibly the most complex element of codification of expertise, far more so than learning the technology itself, as it is not how we have been taught to think or prefer to work. For this to be successful, the expertise and its associated rules need to be captured as a description of a topic instead of as processes to determine an outcome. This can be a challenge for professionals who have been through an education system based on outcomes and then find themselves in a workplace that focuses on deploying scale tactics via linear processes. However, it is the ability to focus on why something is the way it is that gives artificial intelligence the flexibility it needs to deploy human expertise in a situational way.

The second tier in this process is the technology itself, particularly the deployment of inference-based knowledge graphs for determining the expertise that has been captured. The first tier has the knowledge but does not answer any questions; the second tier is inference, which can be applied over the top to take that expertise and use it like a map of a city to begin navigating its way towards an output. Ask it to direct you to a destination (a decision the knowledge should be able to get you to) and it will use the expertise, data from external sources, and human interaction when required, to find its way to the correct and most efficient outcome. In this example, experts are capturing the "rules of the road" for their topic and the technology is finding the fastest and most appropriate route to an answer.

Bridging the gap between machine learning and robotics

The great thing about these technologies, and why I reference them as sitting between the current understanding of robotics and the potential of machine learning, is that it has the best of both. It can infer from a very wide overview of the challenge (decision) being posed to it. It behaves just like machine learning, but at its core, it is based on rules that are explainable to anyone who wants to see the outcome without needing to understand code just like robotics.

In an exceptionally crowded new technology and automation marketplace, these capabilities are a fresh focus for industry as they become aware of the possibilities that can be unlocked with this kind of automation. However, the word "new" is perhaps misplaced in this context. Intelligent automation has a firm place in areas in need of such capabilities and is in production across multiple markets. Intelligent automation has historically supported fraud investigation, healthcare insurance decisions, complex tax analysis, and credit determinations globally.

The combination of human potential and artificial intelligence

Businesses that are focused on knowledge management are ripe for codification on this basis because, if for no other reason, knowledge is an asset that organizations are persistently at risk of losing. People, along with their skill, expertise, and competence are always at risk of leaving a business and taking their knowledge with them. This risk is greater now in our post-pandemic world than it ever has been before.

Codification of specialisms and scarce expertise allows such knowledge and hard earnt experience to be preserved and used, should your experts decide to vacate. In addition, personal expertise can be transformed into organizational expertise and utilized in a scaled format across organizations. What we are referring to here is not the codification of the rules or processes a company owns, although that is often also included, but instead the tacit expertise of how to apply those rules and processes to achieve high-quality organizational results. Essentially, your best minds are codified, scaled, and made available to everyone.

Organizations have a mixture of written and unwritten expertise and both can be easily merged and deployed in a highly consultative and situational manner. This means that the use of the knowledge is seemingly identical to asking a specialist for a view on a topic and giving the specifics of the case at hand to initiate a better response. This use of knowledge is uniformed into a repository of information that your best individuals have to offer, all tied in accordance with the policies of the organization, regulatory requirements, and situational specifics.

Imagine for a second that you have to solve a task. You have available all of the data your organization has access to, and an automated version of the best people in the business. Imagine further that, within a timeline of sub-seconds, all of that has been applied to your scenario (with you providing the intricate details) to determine the best way forwards.

The reason we are now in a time where this is possible is that we have taken a leap of faith in accepting that humans are good at some things and machines are good at others. Success is about being more open and accepting about this, and ensuring that each partner embarks on the most suitable tasks. Some examples of this include:

- *Noise*. Humans are great at adapting to situations that can be both positive and negative. However, a side effect of such adaptability means that other tasks outside the "noise" (external factors) are vulnerable to error and inconsistency. Machines, however, are great at deploying uniformity at scale without distraction and are not affected by external forces unless asked to be.
- *Consistency*. Humans are great at specifying rules. We have been educated and trained to do so for each other and for technology, but machines are great at pointing out inconsistencies in any such rules and looking at them in a truly holistic manner.

- *Local vs global.* Humans like to see themselves as global beings, yet excel only when tracking rules locally. Machines, however, are great at tracking rules globally and forecasting their effects with ease.
- *Interpretable and trustworthy.* Humans are great at explaining why they took short and simple actions, whereas machines are great at explaining compounded actions and laying out how we got to an outcome, regardless of the complexity.
- *Patterns.* Machines are great at generating patterns, while humans are great at identifying the most meaningful and enhancing them. Likewise, humans are great at creating ontologies of things they know and understand, while machines are great at computation within those ontologies at speed and at scale.

The focus of this chapter has been to highlight that the previously untouched areas of complex expertise can now be automated and how in some cases artificial intelligence can be used to enhance processes in ways that were previously considered too difficult or complex.

In this case, the focus has been on a specific, newly recognized, inference-driven element of such technologies but the truth is that no single piece of technology is perfectly suited for automating the entirety of any organizational structure. When we think about the essential power of knowledge that organizations hold, we also need to take into account the data, personal or company information, and the appropriate application methods. It is a case of combining all of these core elements together to create a desirable outcome for an organization.

Technology ecosystems that support business growth

We already know that siloes are a human issue that tech cannot solve alone, and the same is true of any single technology. Therefore, an ecosystem approach is vital to the implementation of such solutions, which is made up of a culmination of digital infrastructures, data for insights, and an augmented human team that is represented both through interaction with systems and by a codification of expertise. Only then can decisions be fed through the matrix with the level of confidence required.

The digital ecosystem is just the first step. Moving forwards with the basics is how many organizations, regardless of size, have taken opportunities to be "digital-first". These teams are focused and more willing to allow technology to assist or orchestrate repetitive decision-making processes, a trust exercise that has rewarded them with competitive advantage. All are supported by the lesser adopted data and predictive insights system options and then all brought together through the melding of human and machine. This process is seamless, with hand-offs in both directions where appropriate.

The final piece of the puzzle when it comes to the ecosystem approach is to not forget that seamless human and machine systems need to be easily usable. Both artificial intelligence and automation have a natural kinship in service design and agile build delivery methods. Therefore, an iterative approach is both possible and reasonable to achieve when capturing expertise for reuse at scale.

As a result, these technologies can be tested or built on lower budgets and easily scaled to meet need or demand. Service design helps develop the concept of a minimal viable proposition as an initial creation, this being a topic or part of a service that can demonstrate an immediate benefit on a small scale. This is important when codifying specific human expertise to avoid it being a labor-intensive process and therefore a barrier to use.

Because the application of such technologies is still considered by many to be exploratory, projects are often required to start on a small scale and align with innovation or process improvement budgets rather than IT budgets, although this shift towards the latter is occurring more often as ideas turn into production systems for enterprises.

Large organizations, such as those in banking or professional services, have invested more in AI than most, but are still in the trial phases for the majority of tasks and production phases for only a few. They will initially try to review the potential of the technologies on a low level and opt to tackle elements where there is an existing, but not regulatory-bound, challenge.

Establishing trust in AI to deliver business value

All elements mentioned here are helpful, but the future rests in the hands of pioneering organizations that properly adopt the connection of some or all of these elements to increase the quality of performance within ecosystems of automation.

In knowledge management projects, it is common for the value generated from technology systems to not be a stand-alone saving, but to be worked into a more significant business case or treated as an enabler. Traditional automation needs volume to be applied for a business case to work, and artificial intelligence alone requires large amounts of data and caseload information before measurable value can emerge. That being said, an ecosystem approach can reach exercises of greater value without a sizable build, and business cases improve in tandem.

Overall, this presents a compelling case for AI spending against a number of key and achievable goals. Leading to far more traditional and tangible benefits as progression occurs, ecosystems of intelligent automation can work in alignment with specific expectations that organizations consider to be valuable.

Chapter 8:
Search

By Jon Beaumont, senior manager of knowledge management, Shearman & Sterling LLP

Introduction

With the advancement of legal technology and related systems over the past 20 years, it is logical to believe that the ability to create, capture, store, and retrieve knowledge within a law firm has become a straightforward process. However, even with the pandemic providing increased value in remote or more systematic focused sharing and collaboration, these various facets of KM are not always as simple to approach as may be thought. In this chapter, I will be examining the search portion of the knowledge process, reviewing approaches to locating knowledge, data, systems, users, solutions, results, and possible future advancements. I shall help to understand what lawyers may be looking for and why, examining the methods that have been employed to achieve a more successful search experience.

Previously

Historically, law firms largely used to operate with a core set of standard and approved "crown jewel" precedents, which were usually easy to locate as they were centralized at the forefront of any particular system (if not still in paper format!). Amendments to these documents were cumbersome and may have even had an extended approval process, resulting in a senior lawyer (possibly even the managing or senior partner) having final sign off on the most minuscule of changes. Whilst this may differ per firm, it tended to be a fairly common experience and obviously didn't account for the fact that lawyers do not simply need documents at the start of a matter or that any new business might not be similar enough to require the same set of materials. However, it was often underlined to junior lawyers that such documents needed to be their start point, whatever the transaction. I recall one "maverick" partner informing me that there was no need for any sort of systematic knowledge capture as he "began each matter with a blank sheet of paper and a pencil". Whilst such a reinvention of materials is seemingly wasteful, I do understand that some matters cannot necessarily be completely pre-defined, although the argument for better KM of course (inclusive of search), is to be able to commoditize the commoditizable.

What is knowledge?

With the understanding in later years that it was not only this core set of documents that could be useful and constitute "knowledge", a greater focus was placed on content and its retrieval. What also arose was the fact that it wasn't just documents that could formulate knowledge within a firm, but practically anything that assisted with any operation, whether this was client or financial data or the experience of a firm's own lawyers. With the rise in knowledge came the need for better storage methods for increased volumes of materials and therefore a heavier emphasis on search and not browse.

Location and content

Before looking at the approaches to search, it is important to understand the different locations of knowledge within law firms and where differences have originated. Whilst it is arguable that this should no longer matter (lawyers still expect a Google experience, no matter how much time we spend discussing this with them and the minimal contribution we receive towards development), there are many challenges that make this possibility rather difficult (security being one fundamental restraint here).

Where is data and knowledge held in law firms?

Historically, location would largely involve separate or duplicative locations for knowledge away from the original source, but the manual nature of moving material would dissuade some from this option. However, one huge benefit to this is the creation of a workflow that not only sees the re-location of knowledge, but also an approval or moderation process for that knowledge. In a risk adverse profession, this can be seen as a big driver, with any knowledge having been "approved" seen as worthwhile.

Types of knowledge

It would be fairly usual to consider that a firm's main "type" of knowledge would be contained in either expertise/experience, financials, or matters. As mentioned, the location (largely putting aside tacit knowledge for this chapter) for these areas will be paramount to search, particularly the number of systems we may need to search to return useful results (Document

Management System (DMS), Matter Management System (MMS), intranet, deal rooms, case management systems, conferencing platforms, client portals, Microsoft Teams, transaction management platforms, Customer Relationship Management (CRM) etc.). It is often considered the case that the smaller number of separate repositories the better, but that may be questionable depending on what an organization is trying to achieve. Realistically it would be a challenge to search all potential knowledge. It is also important to understand the sorts of data we are attempting to retrieve, for example, are we dealing with structured or unstructured data, the latter of which may provide different challenges.

Bringing together results from different systems and providing them to an individual in a meaningful way is certainly demanding. There could potentially be no direct comparison between sets of data, whether that's in the approval process (or lack of) or a consolidation of data that should not be merged due to its substantive and fundamental difference. Data sets largely need to have some comparable value or at least a single shared point, which largely within firms has been the universally understood client-matter number. Would there be any point in displaying different sets of data without any relevant comparisons (for example, where knowledge may have shared fields)? Should documents that had been "approved" as part of a particular workflow be highlighted as such against a post on an internal Teams site? Is there a hierarchy of source material; for example, would we trust a financial system or new business intake process more than we would trust other sources? The questions raised show that source location is significant to a user if searching multiple locations, and possibly the burden should be on that individual to make their own judgment on its validity. The consolidation of knowledge can confuse a user and may not always be the correct method.

Another important question that arises is the relationship of data. For example, does a "matter location" have the exact same meaning throughout systems? If not, this would certainly cause an issue. Holistic mapping of data and its flows becomes paramount, and many firms now employ individuals to manage this aspect with firmwide data dictionaries commonplace. Such a team will often be responsible for this area and also mapping various system integrations (which can be surprisingly difficult indeed).

Basic approaches

There are certainly systems currently provided by vendors on the market that allow search across single and multiple knowledge sources, but this is often aided by providing additional metadata to reside on a piece of knowledge. The use of keywords and tags has been considered somewhat archaic, but it is still relevant in a number of firms in assisting search. It can additionally help with workflows related to authorization of knowledge.

Despite the difficulties we can encounter with search, we are seeing many more ingenious methods of trying to provide and push users' results. Outside of legal, such innovative methods of fulfilling search enquiries are commonplace (albeit not necessarily always understood as to "how" by the user), although machine learning and behavioral understanding has proved difficult in the legal environment. It's often that lawyers don't care about unknown contributions to better search in their personal life but have a very different view on any tracking at work. The "uniqueness" of the lawyering role is often used as a diversion by lawyers, but a reticence to allow insight can restrict what can be provided by search, particularly if behaviors are never truly understood.

Keywords and tagging

The use of taxonomies for tagging documents to allow categories of results to be provided to a user is still surprisingly commonplace, and despite advancements and changes in our technologies it is a method that can prove extremely useful. One large positive is the fact that lawyers understand and trust such an approach. The trust factor once again probably being related to the fact that an individual has applied such a tag. Having a robust and flexible taxonomy helps enormously here, with this approach allowing lawyers to provide searchable metadata that may not be contained in any of the document content (and thus not providing results for their search). For example, any method of applying a document type, an industry, location, or party roles on a matter for internal knowledge is undoubtedly helpful. The downside is the time taken for this manual approach, consistency (in naming and interpretation of values), practice/geographical differences, and arguments around the taxonomies themselves.

Expectations

Expectations amongst lawyers remain high in that they believe they should be able to locate any piece of knowledge they require in a single search. As mentioned previously, merging search results from different systems is not without its issues and whilst enterprise search is certainly possible, it's an area that law firms have struggled with. A lawyer doesn't want to be locating a matter with transactional details from one system to then populate different systems with those results to see financials, deal teams, and documents. Further, a lawyer largely does not know that a document search with matter details on an MMS is not going to redeem much in the way of useful documentation (if anything at all). From a lawyer perspective, shouldn't they be able to search in one place and see everything they need?

Knowledge, data, and systems

In discussing the approach to knowledge and data for search, I should underline that we are largely considering structured data here. Furthermore, we are assuming that the majority of data is of a reasonable standard, as no search tool is going to remedy bad data (as yet), although we can see data being made at least more beneficial by some processes.

Data flow

Reverting back to the location of knowledge, it's obviously essential for any tool to be aware of this and able to index fully what is required, regardless of physical location or system. We need to be aware too of system-to-system population and data flows and make sure that we are focused upon the correct place. Population of systems throughout the new business intake process is a common example of this and understanding which financial, matter, document, or external products are populated and by what is obviously fundamental to search.

Many firms will now have in place a hub/lake/shelter where data is stored agnostic of a system, which is very helpful for search and often allows us to view the source of truth for data. It is fine to have data flowing across systems of course (in fact, this is encouraged and largely how best to leverage internal data), but it is vital that the system of reference is known, and if data can be entered in different systems, that this in turn populates elsewhere where relevant. Such data movement provides the possible systematic injection of certain metadata, for example if particular rules are met.

Integrations

We often see numerous system integrations within law firms, particularly those of a historical nature. Integrations obviously allow some extremely useful flows across systems (pulling externally as well as internally), but experience has shown that field naming across systems is often not consistent and can lead to several labels for the same piece of data. Thus, when configuring search, it is essential to make sure that we are absolutely explicit in our work. The fundamental question of "What am I searching?" is so important here, as too is the future proofing of any search tool, with understanding of short-, medium-, and long-term objectives of a project and in tandem any plans for development or change to relevant systems. There should also be an intelligent plan for storage and flows of data to lessen problems with system replacement if this is not already the case.

User experience

Obviously, the majority of systems will provide their own inherent search functionality, which is now usually excellent. If I was to search the vast majority of law firm standard DMS or MMS with relevant search data, I'm sure that I would be able to locate pretty much anything I am looking for. Nevertheless, therein lies the issue that the searcher largely has to know which system to use to reap the best (or even any!) results.

As stated, the downside of having different systems for different data in legal (and this is certainly not a complaint about vendors) is that lawyers do not want to be searching in multiple locations for knowledge. Historically, vendors competed with in-house solutions to provide search on what were on-premises systems. With the introduction and success of cloud platforms for law firms, the emphasis now has been on vendor assistance for enterprise search. With this shift in solutions comes a different support and cost model, which is certainly necessary to understand when engaging with vendors in this relatively new area.

Having mentioned the difficulty of mapping some of the firm's systems and integrations, it is easy to forget what benefits can be found. Not only are we considering bringing in external knowledge sources such as documents, but standardized lists for the legal sector and also available matter information, which supersedes internal necessity to populate information within our own systems. With standardization we are talking about excellent work taking place by organizations in the US and UK (and elsewhere) to standardize terminology for matters across the legal sector, which can then be leveraged. External matter data may provide the ability to understand corporate structures, locations, industry, and non-client organizations alongside our own content, which then becomes fully searchable. This takes away at least some of the data entry from teams and ensures a high standard of knowledge.

Challenges

In a global law firm, further issues can surround non-English language documents, which can prove challenging to index and therefore retrieve.

The rise in more informal communication between lawyers internally and their clients externally can also create difficulties. This is not only in how to approach potential knowledge value in WhatsApp correspondence and MS Teams chat, but the effect of any retention/deletion processes that surround such mediums and the ramifications on search.

Users and solutions

Any initial focus on improvement of search has to understand significantly the user requirements. In law firms, where time is such a scarce commodity for lawyers, it can be extremely difficult to completely understand these requirements. Developing search on the basis of our own understanding would not usually work either. I have already referenced the amount of requests from lawyers that search should look and operate "like Google", but digging into this, what does it actually mean? Putting Google aside, what is it that they want to achieve?

Requirements

From the lawyers I have engaged with, I feel there are four main requirements. First, as discussed, they want a single search over all relevant knowledge repositories, which is potentially possible now, but will become more realistic and advanced in time. This requirement will more deeply cover the ability to search for a particular knowledge type (e.g., documents) with virtually any information they may have. Again, possible to a certain extent.

Second, they want clean, reliable and precise data that is accessible to them immediately. Challenges such as verification of knowledge and security (covered later) are never really considered by lawyers and rather than a search problem, this relates back to a firm's process for knowledge (if indeed there is one) and security model.

Third, they want the ability to use results that are relevant in a pertinent way. This could be the amendment of a basic Word precedent document once located or automated use of experience and matter data that is transferred to PowerPoint for a pitch.

Finally, and one as owners of search (if indeed the team are responsible for the search tools) that has been a constant struggle, is the personalization of a user's results. The expectation that a single search term can provide hugely relevant results for an individual is a gigantic challenge that involves defining usefulness from a multitude of knowledge mediums across many systems. User interaction with results has historically been minimal too, either in liking/favoriting results or providing feedback systematically or in-person (outside of the common "search doesn't work"). So, what approaches do we have at our disposal to improve personalization with minimal lawyer input?

Filtering

One of the powerful inclusions in a number of systems has been the much-improved use of filters. Used heavily outside of the legal world, these allow a potentially general search to be narrowed quickly and effectively by the user with practically any further detail they have. Examples within an MMS may be in relation to a work type, industry or location and within a DMS, file type, practice group, or author. Filtering will undoubtedly play a huge role in search (as illogical as that may sound), particularly in enterprise search where a lawyer may be looking for documents or a document type, but also wants to search with matter metadata (a very common approach). The ability to search within filters themselves only adds to their value.

I have witnessed some reticence amongst lawyers to use filtering, which seems to be a lack of trust around what they are actually filtering (and thus excluding), coupled with the inherent fear that something may be missed if results are narrowed. This leads to large results lists and a general frustration around search.

User journey and relevancy

Lawyers tend to have a similar mistrust in allowing access to their behavior in searching. So, what can be done to better try and fulfil a lawyer's requirements of relevancy in search? There is some basic individual data that can be used initially to try and assist here, such as a searcher's practice group, which could be used as an initial parameter to only search knowledge of that particular team. Similarly, we could extend this understanding of an individual to see which matters they have worked upon, which documents they have previously accessed, previous search terms they have used, and similar searches and knowledge that have been utilized by their team (usually found in the storage system itself). If a law firm has its own experience/expertise repository, this could be leveraged for greater understanding and weighting of areas that may be relevant to the particular individual searching.

Further, we could look to weight certain types of results for individuals or groups. Such relevancy tuning is often possible but weighting of one aspect of knowledge can sometimes have a negative effect on relevancy of other meaningful knowledge. It's a fine line that can absorb a great deal of time with no great value.

A number of legal technology providers have developed new methods of locating data relevant to an individual. This has sometimes been with a specific task in mind as opposed to a more universal search tool. However, when examining some of the natural language processing approaches (language patterns as opposed to keywords) or search utilized with e-Discovery in mind, the applicability to knowledge search (particularly with the latter) is an interesting one. Additionally, would there be solutions here for some of the manual processes like tagging in future? For example, if a common or specific type of document could be recognized, it could then be tagged with useful search metadata without any human interaction.

Results

The systematic difficulty in being able to consolidate search results in a meaningful way have been outlined. But what about the presentation of such results?

Positives

It appears that this area is less difficult, with vendors offering full design of the user interface (UI), positioning results and other further search possibilities (filters, advanced search etc.) pretty much wherever an organization decides. What hasn't been largely possible as yet is the individual ability to fully customize the UI. Despite the ability for customization at an administrative level, lawyers do tend to want items in a particular location or to be displayed in a specific way (which may not necessarily always be consistent or seem logical).

In addition to UI enhancements, small developments have made for a hugely more rewarding experience recently. The ability to use type-ahead in search, tailored and valuable suggestions, clear distinctions regarding what and where an individual is searching, search history, preview, export (users not only have the ability to export or print a piece of knowledge, but lists of results for sharing or further manipulation are easily produced), and clear advanced search (which historically was even considered to only be applicable to IT or system administrative individuals!) has made search a fundamentally more worthwhile experience.

Challenges

One recurring issue that should be flagged is the use of search results amongst lawyers. As mentioned previously, security is paramount to law firms, which has led to many implementing pessimistic rather than optimistic security models for systems. In this case, data is restricted to groups or individuals initially and can be opened wider as opposed to data being accessible to all within a firm and having to be restricted where appropriate (or when individuals remember to do it). Sharing results within a matter team should therefore usually be possible but sharing outside of that matter team may not. Further, certain content may be restricted for access but viewable in results (a client or document name for example), but in some models a user will not even be able to see anything regarding a result to which they do not have access. It's important that this is understood when configuring search. It may be that a firm believes it useful to see a result even if it is not accessible, but this shouldn't be possible if any sort of confidentiality is breached in any way. This can cause confusion and frustration, although the security model is largely operating as intended. One approach is to somehow group restricted data where applicable as "knowledge" and thus exclude it from the usual security provisions. This returns to the idea of curation of certain data. Any model will require thorough and comprehensive review, but search should not be seen as a way to navigate around security. It is absolutely fundamental that search can replicate all security of any given system.

Analytics

Analytics regarding search have advanced hugely, and it is certainly advantageous to be able to view and utilize "user journeys" to advance and develop search. General feedback from users is sometimes useful, but it is equally important to be able to validate this with analytics. Much can be seen from the way a lawyer approaches searching for knowledge.

Education

Finally, as regards results, the ability to "train" users will undoubtedly arise. Often, from a lawyer's perspective, search should be so intuitive that any guidance on how to use it would not even be needed. It is probably agreeable that search should be intuitive and maybe previous classroom methods of training lawyers are not necessarily warranted and certainly not the best approach. Nevertheless, I do still feel that it is important to provide guidance on the capabilities and best practice as lawyers are not going to take the time to learn themselves. It is often now a discussion with an internal training team as how to provide materials and such guidance when assisting with search.

The future

We may conclude that there is not currently a perfect method, process, or technology that can deliver 100 percent of what may be required for search within law firms and maybe we shall never reach that nirvana. However, the signs of a much more useful search experience for lawyers are increasingly positive and if the challenges outlined can be addressed, I believe we shall have some hugely valuable developments that can assist with meeting expectations. With the continued use of better categorization for knowledge (including the replacement of manual processes, along with beneficial, consistent, and meaningful taxonomies), less-siloed storage, personalization, and use of learning where applicable, search can really be as valuable to lawyers as we know it should be.

Chapter 9:
Digital transformation, knowledge management, and cybersecurity in the post-COVID era

By Tiffany M. O'Neil, director of KM and technology innovation, and James G. Perkins, chief operating officer and chief compliance officer, Procopio, Cory, Hargreaves & Savitch LLP

Introduction

In this chapter we discuss at a strategic overview level the use of technology in law firms, the path the industry was on regarding the digital transformation of their business before the COVID-19 pandemic, and where it is now positioned coming out of the pandemic (termed the post-COVID era). Technology has numerous categories and components but for the sake of this chapter we focus on knowledge management (KM), cybersecurity, and the business models used to position technology within the law firm "industry". We discuss digital transformation as if it has been readily accepted as the way forward by the industry although we acknowledge that firms will be at very different phases of such a transformation, the idea of digital mastery, the typical software in the knowledge management ecosystem, technological innovation by law firms, and cybersecurity. The concept of "Managing on the Edge"™ also re-surfaces.[1]

As mentioned in a chapter I wrote for another publication on profitability,[2] our firm, like many regional firms in the country, plans to stay independent and as such needs to hold its own in the battles against our main competitors who are not only strong and innovative California firms, but also national and global firms. We have to date been very successful in this endeavor in the main because several years ago we embraced a management philosophy we term Managing on the Edge™. Managing on the Edge™ makes us focus on those activities "on the margin" that bring small positive incremental changes. These incremental changes when added together can make a substantial difference to the bottom line. As discussed in that chapter, these incremental activities are mostly economic and directly affect the financials of the firm; however, other activities such as allowing clients a secure window into our business intelligence data or our collaborations with the Ritz Carlton Leadership Center to improve client service, have an indirect but long-term effect on our bottom line. Technology fits into being an activity that can have significant indirect positive impact on a firm's economical health and client satisfaction. Becoming a technology leader is the latest and potentially most important Managing on the Edge™ incremental activity, and we can certainly state that the pandemic has accelerated our move along the digital transformation path.

Digital mastery

Law firms and the legal industry in general are not known for their prowess in technology. The majority of law firms are partnerships of one sort or another, and in a partnership "cash is king", and the spending of every expense dollar is done reluctantly as the owners/shareholders/equity partners realize that an additional dollar spent means that their compensation pool at year-end will be reduced by that amount. Thus, using technology to transform their business model has not been a priority for law firms, so before we discuss knowledge management and cybersecurity we need to review where firms are positioned regarding technology and we need to get a sense of where law firms sit in what we would term the technology ecosystem.

In their 2014 book, *Leading Digital – Turning Technology Into Business Transformation*, George Westerman, Didier Bonnet, and Andrew McAfee outlined a simple approach to positioning industries in a matrix of "digital capability" and "leadership capability".[3] Figure 1 shows such positioning with one additional point, that of law firms, added by the authors. Our positioning is not from any scientific analysis or surveys but what we feel is a reasonable assumption from our knowledge gained over the years from working with our peer firms. Westerman et al coined four levels of "digital mastery" – *Beginners, Fashionistas, Conservatives*, and the crème de la crème, *Digital Masters*.

Westerman et al's research showed a striking performance difference for Digital Masters versus the rest in revenue generation efficiency, earnings, profitability, and net profit margin. They quote that, on average, Digital Masters are 26 percent more profitable than their industry competitors and they generate nine percent more revenue.[4] Thus, it seems that embracing digital transformation can, and often does, lead to a stronger financial performance and more potential opportunities in the marketplace. Building both digital and leadership capabilities makes very good business sense regardless of industry, and law firms should embrace the program to become closer to being a Digital Master. Being a Digital Master means that a law firm needs to:

- Embrace a strong digital vision and believe that the increased use of technology will improve the overall client delivery experience as well as improve the firm's financial performance;
- Have excellent governance across all departments, offices, practice groups, and industry groups;
- Have many digital initiatives generating business value in measurable ways; and
- Develop a strong digital culture.

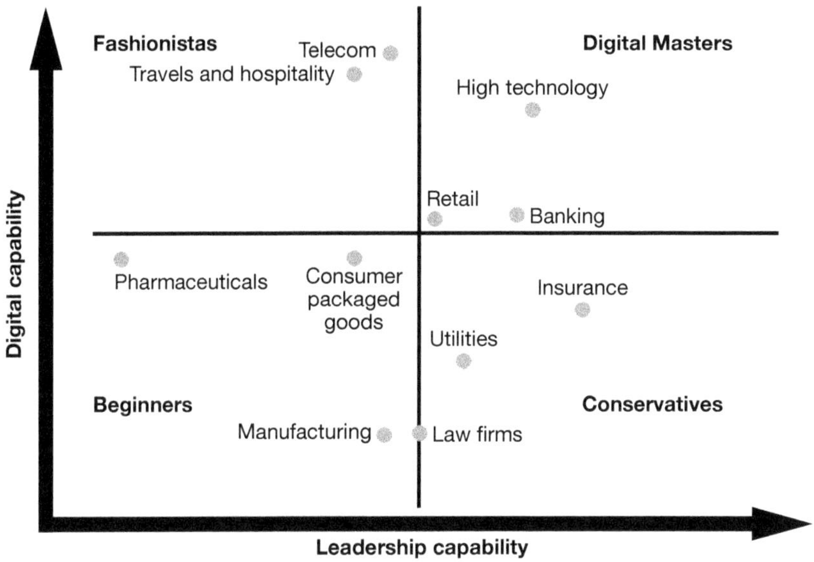

Figure 1: Digital Mastery by Industry. Source: Adapted from Westerman, G., Bonnet, D., and McAfee, A., Leading Digital – Turning Technology Into Business Transformation, *Harvard Business Review Press, Boston, MA, 2014.*

We are convinced that to be able to continue to be competitive and survive the future, all law firms, regardless of their present position, need to move toward the upper right of Figure 1 and into the Digital Masters level.

We can also look at digital transformation in the legal industry through the Susskind Grid, originally developed by Richard Susskind.[5] An adaption is shown in Figure 2. Again, we see four quadrants with the Y-axis delineating a focus from the Internal (in-house IS department etc.) at the bottom to the External (clients) at the top, and the X-axis focusing on technology/data to the left information/knowledge to the right. Our goal is to be heavily engaged in the top right quadrant where we are sharing information and knowledge with clients, working with them through secure and seamless collaborative sites and, where appropriate, developing processes and programs for their own use. Being heavily involved in the top right-hand quadrant is akin to being in the Digital Master quadrant of the Digital Mastery Matrix.

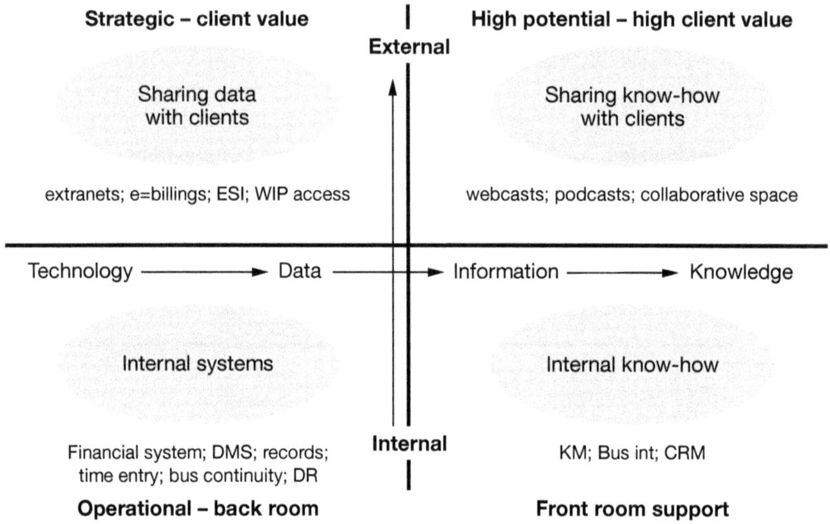

Figure 2: Leveraging Technology – The Susskind Grid. Source: Adapted from Susskind, R., Transforming the Law: Essays on Technology, Justice and the Legal Marketplace, *Oxford University Press, 2010.*

A third way we like to look at where law firms are in the digital transformation space is to use S-Curve charts,[6] which is one of our favorite business tools in strategic planning. Figure 3 shows a conceptual positioning of where we estimate law firms are in relation to technology. An S-Curve[7] is a graph of the relationship between the effort put into improving a product, service, or process and the results one gets back for that investment and/or time. It's called an S-Curve because when the results are plotted, what usually appears is a sinuous line shaped like a S, but pulled to the right at the top and pulled to the left at the bottom. Initially the product, service, or process develops slowly, then as the knowledge to advance is put in place there is a significant acceleration and then finally as the product etc. matures it becomes more expensive to make advances and the curve starts to plateau and eventually will decline unless new ideas or initiatives are put in place for a new S-Curve to develop upwards again.

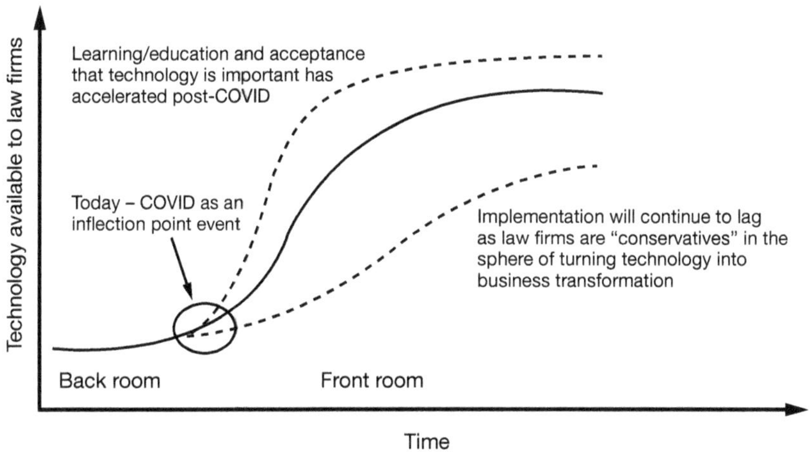

Figure 3: Technology in Law Firms – Where are we today? Source: Adapted from Foster, R., Innovation – The Attacker's Advantage, *"The S-Curve: A New Forecasting Tool", Summit Books, New York, 1986.*

We do not think that pre-COVID law firms had reached the inflexion point to start the speedy advance up the S-Curve. We were "just at that point" in 2019/2020, in our view. The pandemic though has, in our opinion, seriously positioned law firms to start moving up two separate S-Curves – one we can call the "learning/education and acceptance that technology is very important" S-Curve and the other, the "implementation" S-Curve. As shown in Figure 3, we think that the learning/education curve has moved fast during COVID-19, but the implementation curve, while moving upwards, will be at a much slower pace. To quote my colleague and consultant Ralph Baxter, advisor to law firms and legal technology companies, and former chairman and CEO at Orrick, Herrington and Sutcliffe:

> *"Following the pandemic there has been a significant increase in firm awareness of the benefit to be derived from information technology to improve nearly every facet of firm operations. Firms don't have clear ideas of what they want in terms of tools, but they have an appetite to make more of their collective knowledge and other information, and recognize that technology can help them make the most of it."*[8]

Law firms realize that they need technology but are still figuring out the best way to implement it. As Conservative in the Digital Mastery Matrix, they have a Technology Gap! In a 2019 private survey conducted globally by a major legal software provider, this technology gap was obvious with 80 to 90 percent of law firms believing that improved automation and information was very important but only 15 to 20 percent actively developing solutions.[9] Of more concern was that, in the same survey, 40 to 50 percent of clients were expecting to have a modern digital experience in the very near future.

Knowledge management and technology innovation

KM is a broad term that means different things to different firms. At our firm we have been handling KM for many years in the "Back Room". Through our Back Room systems – document management, ESI (electronically stored information) systems, financial systems, HR systems etc. – we can satisfactorily access all the historical knowledge developed by our attorneys in a relatively speedy fashion, most via immediate access. Via our practice teams, practice groups, and industry groups, relevant industry or technical information can be easily shared. This type of KM does not move the needle to those upper right quadrants on our Digital Mastery Matrix or Susskind Grid. To do that we need technological innovation and in order to implement that, we created, in 2019, a Technology Innovation Group (TIG), initially staffed by several members from the central Information Services (IS) department. The staff was subsequently augmented by programmers and data scientists hired externally. The TIG reports up to the COO through the director of KM and technology innovation, not through the director of IS. It is technological innovations, offered to both partners and attorneys internally as well as to clients, through TIG that will move the firm up the S-Curve, into the "Front Room", and to the Digital Master space.

The main purpose of TIG is fourfold:

- To research, evaluate, develop, and implement where appropriate various AI technology products that improve user workflows and increase efficiency;
- To develop incremental efficiencies on internal processes via discreet projects, many processes driven by data spreadsheets;
- Using specific third party software to develop programs for collaboration with both clients and internal practice teams and practice and industry groups; and
- To train the appropriate end users on key new TIG products and processes.

TIG manages all the new AI-enabled KM products and services like Westlaw, Lexis, Lex Machina, Patent Optimizer, Patent Advisor, Docket Navigator, Drafting Assistant (Litigation and Transactional), and Relativity, and we are presently beta-testing ThoughtTrace. Using third party development software, TIG has built, deployed, and maintained over 200 active deal room type sites for various internal practice teams and groups and almost 100 active external client-facing sites.

Cybersecurity

This chapter has focused on the digital transformation of law firms and their business models, or maybe the lack of it; however, behind every digital transformation lies the protection needed for all digital activities – that is the subject of cybersecurity. Cybersecurity takes a continued, and usually increasing, annual investment (at about 2.5 to 4 percent of revenue) in technology to combat the external threats all businesses face. That investment is a substantial amount of money and, as we indicated in the introduction, in law firm partnerships there is always reluctance to spend money when the return is not obvious. At Procopio we have had a long-standing commitment to a strong technology security program, being one of the earliest law firms to buy into the first cyber insurance policies that were available out of the London insurance market. The onset of the pandemic did accelerate slightly some of the risk prevention aspects of cybersecurity, especially with regard to the "human error" potential. Many of the data breaches that are experienced by business come from this "human error" component and it is that component that is often ignored or to which not enough attention is paid. Some examples of stepped up programs we enacted due to COVID-19 were:

- At the start of the "work at home" orders in March 2020 we had all attorneys and staff sign new remote working agreements that covered their responsibilities on security, client confidentiality, and practice management.
- In June 2020, when we realized that work at home was going to extend for a longer time period than initially thought, we made sure that all attorneys and staff had all the necessary encrypted laptops, double monitors, internet connections, printers, scanners, shredders, and communication devices to ensure they could work at home as seamlessly as at the office. These expenditures have become a key part of our annual technology budget.

- With attorneys and staff working in a solo environment due to the pandemic lockdowns (numerous in California), we realized early the security vulnerabilities that would come from these remote/isolation situations. However, using our proprietary Virtual Desktop (VDI) allowed every user, attorney, and staff, to be connected as if in the office, being able to share screens and view documents in real time and work together on production of documents. In March 2020 we transitioned seamlessly to all attorneys and staff working remotely in a matter of 72 hours, with full security preserved. Review and supervision of work product continued as before, just as if all involved were in the office.
- We put a major focus on all training on confidentiality. All were trained to watch participants in virtual conference rooms, use passwords and waiting rooms where appropriate. All conflict checks and review capabilities were easily accessed with mobile applications. In essence there was nothing we could do in the office that could not be done remotely as far as work product was concerned.

We have had many of our lawyers travel extensively for many years, especially due to our growing Latin America and Asian practices, so it was not new for attorneys to work remotely. Because of that extensive travel overseas we developed in the mid-2000s a very secure proprietary Virtual Desktop System and implemented procedures via encrypted laptops that, as stated above, allowed an attorney to be in exactly the same system and screen views remotely just as if they were at their office computers. While this chapter is not intended to be a detailed list of technology systems and software, it might be useful to outline how during COVID-19 we re-positioned our security systems to protect against malicious attacks and ransomware in particular.

Protecting against attacks

While we have many facets of technology in place to help protect against malicious intruders, there are four main ways we approach such threats:

1. Blocking access to get inside our systems.
2. If an intruder is already inside, preventing the attack from executing.
3. If the attack is able to execute, alert our IT department and other security personnel of the current attack to enable immediate countermeasures.

4. If the ransomware attack was successful, make sure we could recover encrypted files from an air gapped and immutable backup system.

For blocking access we have in place:

- Next generation firewalls;
- Two factor authentication (MFA) for remote and office access to our Virtual Desktop and Outlook Web Access;
- Access blocked from "Known Bad Actor" countries with a large database that is kept updated in real time from over a dozen international government and NGO databases;
- Mail gateways that block malware and malicious web links;
- Software to protect against public-facing web applications; and
- Regular penetration testing and vulnerability assessments that are carried out on a regular basis by third party expert companies to uncover any potential vulnerabilities.

The firewalls are constantly updated with enhanced rules from the cloud and use AI to examine traffic to determine whether it is legitimate traffic for the end client or not. These main technologies work at the perimeter to provide protection to prevent an outside intruder from gaining access through brute force.

If an attacker is already inside our systems we prevent attacks from executing by the following.

- Extensive training and testing of all attorneys and staff via online phishing programs. The most probabilistic and realistic threat is through phishing. Whether that's a user giving someone their password on a website, allowing an IT imposter over the phone access to their desktop, or clicking a malicious link, these are the most likely ways a malicious actor would be able to gain access to our systems.
- Whitelisting all applications that are allowed to run on our VDI, checking them against a database that we maintain, which only allows our approved software to run. If it is not in our approved database, then it cannot execute, which would include most, if not all, malicious file types, including any remote access software that an imposter might try to install if they were on the phone phishing a user posing as IT support.

- Using a Non-Persistent Virtual Desktop (VDI), as these don't allow any file write access to the operating system. Any threats that access the operating system during the user's session will be erased with a simple reboot. In other words, every time a machine is rebooted, it comes up as a freshly-made machine, and all files and processes from the last session are erased. This is especially important, because a major ransomware threat that lurks is that if the machine is infected, it can encrypt the hard drive of the user's PC, rendering it useless, and if this is done across hundreds or thousands of machines, it would make for a nightmare to recover and reimage the machines. For us it would just require a simple reboot of the VDI and the problem will be erased.
- Next generation antimalware with best of breed and market leading solution. The software watches all processes for malicious code using AI and their cloud crowdsourcing technology and will block and alert if anything is found. We know that this has already effectively mitigated several real-world threats.

If a malicious actor is able to get past all the controls we have in place, or they are doing no less than drastic measures to take things over, we have other controls in place to alert and help take countermeasures to stop the intrusion. These are:

- Enlisting the services of a company to perform Managed Security Provider (MSP) services, which provides 24/7 monitoring of all system logs and activities;
- An audit system that watches file and email activity and will alert if it sees malicious activity including ransomware based on its AI and rules set, or expected patterns of behavior. We can then investigate and remediate as necessary; and
- Extensive alerting, as almost all network devices on the network are setup for monitoring and can alert individually if they notice any abnormal traffic. Again, we can then investigate and remediate if necessary.

If a ransomware attack was successful, we could recover encrypted files from an air gapped and immutable backup system. An air gapped and immutable backup provides a buffer should a ransomware attack successfully occur. The air gap provides the buffer by taking the regularly backed up data offline and making it unavailable on the network. All scheduled backups are air gapped. The immutable backup is one that cannot be overwritten or modified once the backup copy has been made. It can be used for recovery, but it cannot be overwritten. This type of backup was created specifically for recovering from ransomware scenarios. The immutable backups are tested automatically, which is a feature of the system, to ensure that they have not been encrypted by ransomware.

If, by chance, a malicious intruder happens to get past all the controls in place from above, and able to encrypt a user's files, desktop, or a server, we have multiple avenues of recovery and remediation procedures in place. Files or systems could be restored within minutes. File system previous version copies are created. Whenever a file is modified and saved, the previous version of the file is written to a protected space and written to the file server twice per day. This can be used for quick and easy individual file recovery. We use a Storage Area Network (SAN) as our primary storage system, which has inherent backups taken, called snapshots, at specified intervals. These are offline frozen backups, so they cannot be changed or deleted, but they can be brought up and mounted within minutes to a point in time before they were infected. These snapshots are also replicated to our Disaster Recovery (DR) site in Las Vegas, Nevada and kept on the SAN in that location as well. We also have backup solutions that are in place in the event there are issues with the snapshots on the SAN systems. And the air gapped and immutable backups mentioned above would provide a recovery option.

As a final reminder, all systems, whether they are Back Room, Front Room, or security systems, need to be patched on a regular basis, constantly updated with enhanced rules from the cloud, and AI used to examine traffic to determine whether it is legitimate for the end client or not. These technologies work at the perimeter to provide protection to prevent an outside intruder from gaining access through brute force into any of our systems.

We believe that one of the greatest risks to any system remains users themselves. Phishing and social engineering are the biggest threats to any company, not brute force network entry. During the pandemic we spent a lot of time and energy on improving our online anti-phishing campaigns and security awareness training to educate our personnel. During 2020 and 2021 our total investment in technology (including staff) increased by about seven percent, whereas most data we have seen on law firms in the US shows the overall technology investment per firm stayed static or decreased. We believe it is money well spent.

Conclusion

We believe the pandemic has fast tracked law firms in their learning, education of technology, and their acceptance of the fact that technology is very important. However, the actual implementation of solutions has not increased, continuing to maintain the wide technology gap between law firms' agreement in the necessity of technology improvements and advancements, and their implementation.

We are convinced that to be able to continue to be competitive and survive the future, all law firms, regardless of their present position, need to move toward the goal of becoming, in Westerman et al's words, Digital Masters. At Procopio we believe that the creation of a separate internal Technology Innovation Group, well-staffed and funded, is a key part of achieving that goal and TIG has become one of the most important pieces of our Managing on the Edge™ program. We caution that standard KM activities do not move the needle in the digital transformation of a law firm business and serious technological innovation is required.

With regard to cyber risk, the pandemic accelerated somewhat our training, education of those "human" behaviors that can create risk, notably phishing and social engineering threats. Our committed path to continuously upgrading our protection against cyber-attacks and ransomware did not materially change during COVID-19. Of course, every individual law firm has to make their own decisions on how they invest, to what programs and which personnel and staff. May we respectively suggest that investment in cybersecurity protection is always maintained at the highest level to protect your firm's clients' data.

References

1 Perkins, J.G., "Profitability, the concept of Managing on the Edge, and their importance to a regional law firm", in Bowes, E. (ed.), *The Mechanics of Law Firm Profitability: People, Process and Technology*, London, Ark Group, 2016.

2 *Ibid*.

3 Westerman, G., Bonnet, D., and McAfee, A., *Leading Digital – Turning Technology Into Business Transformation*, Harvard Business Review Press, Boston, MA, 2014.

4 *Ibid*, p18.

5 Susskind, R., *Transforming the Law: Essays on Technology, Justice and the Legal Marketplace*, Oxford University Press, 2010.

6 Foster, R., *Innovation – The Attacker's Advantage*, "The S-Curve: A New Forecasting Tool", Summit Books, New York, 1986; and Barlow, B. "The S-Curve of Business: The Key Levers to Sustaining Momentum for your Brand", Rocketsource.co.

7 *Ibid*.

8 Baxter, R. Private communication.

9 Private survey of global law firms.

Chapter 10:
KM and innovation in law firms and legal departments – twins separated at birth?

By Gordon Vala-Webb, thought leader, speaker/author, and innovation professional

Knowledge management (KM) and innovation, on the face of it, might seem quite dissimilar. The former is often associated with structuring and organizing knowledge while the latter is typically seen as focused on generating and applying new ideas (usually applying new technologies).
It is true that "classical" KM has its roots in collecting and organizing documents. The law library is perhaps the quintessential example of KM in practice within legal organizations, with librarians saying they were doing KM long before KM was invented. And this might seem a long way from new legal tech. However, like fraternal twins, knowledge management and innovation have a great deal of DNA in common.

Who is doing what?

You see some evidence for this in the extraordinary number of legal industry professionals and leaders who have both "knowledge" and "innovation" in their current title. LinkedIn lists almost 100 people who have current titles incorporating both terms (in "legal services" or "law practice" industries).[1] Perhaps the pre-eminent example is Ginevra Saylor – president of the International Legal Technology Association (ILTA) – whose title at the time of writing is national director, innovation and knowledge programs at Gowling WLG (Canada).

It is interesting to note that at the same time LinkedIn only shows roughly 70 people with just "knowledge" in their title in the industry (i.e., without "innovation" in their title). So more have the combined title than just the one term.

Of course, filtering using this combined title does not count the number of people who previously had "knowledge" in their title and now just have "innovation" instead. There has been a veritable "gold rush" into innovation as a role with 1,600 people in our industry on LinkedIn having that term (without "knowledge") in their current title.

Long live KM

So, is KM in legal dying? Or is it a case of "KM is dead, long live KM" in the shape of its fraternal twin – innovation? Arguably this change (transfiguration?) was noticeably accelerated by the move to virtual working as a result of COVID-related office closures. That is, moving all the work of the law firm or legal department into the digital realm dramatically sped-up the change in KM-teams' work from knowledge-focused work to business-change innovation work.

Underpinning this change is that there is a natural – although by no means pre-ordained – progression from doing KM to doing "innovation". You can see this in the career trajectories of those now "innovation" professionals, looking at their work histories on LinkedIn. Unfortunately, it is not possible to use LinkedIn to track that progression at scale (since it would require you to be able to run search results for previous roles versus current ones).

If you look at an individual level, however, typically the journey looks roughly like this: they start by working on KM projects, then they get a role with "knowledge" or "practice support" in their title. As they get more experience – and build more buy-in from their firm or department – they start working on legal technology-related software projects. Finally, they add "innovation" to their title (or replace "knowledge" entirely). You can see this in Ginevra Saylor's work history.

Inter-connections between KM and innovation

So, how are these two disciplines inter-connected? At the most fundamental level, in a professional service firm (or legal department), the core work of the organization is the acquisition and application of specialist knowledge to business problems. This is why many professional service firms of all stripes have historically invested in KM programs, teams, and technology.

This also leads those same organizations to broaden that knowledge management function to include accelerating the uptake of innovative solutions and approaches in those core – knowledge – business processes. Arguably, "innovation" is the search for, and application of, new knowledge to improve the organization's capabilities or service offerings. From this perspective it is appropriate that those who are "managing" knowledge for an organization begin to move from codifying and organizing existing knowledge to helping the organization find and apply new knowledge.

To be clear, in both instances – the organizing (of old) and the exploring (of new) knowledge – are natural and pre-existing organizational activities. No organization could have lasted into the 2020s without some of those capabilities. What knowledge management/innovation functional groups can do is make those efforts more structured, more efficient, more universal, and more effective.

Similarities

Beyond the underlining strategic logic – of optimizing the firm's or department's ability to deliver value within organizations that apply professional expertise – both KM and innovation have many similarities. These include:

- Skillful execution of technology-enabled business projects (tactical perspective);
- Understanding – at a very fundamental level – how your firm or legal department works (operational perspective); and
- Requiring individuals skilled at communicating complex and novel ideas to build the willingness to make change (change management perspective).

It is worth unpacking each of these points in turn.

First, tactically, almost all modern KM projects involve the use of software to enable some part of a business process (e.g., looking up cases as part of legal research). This means KM teams are familiar with the sequence and cadence for software-install projects, along with issues of metadata structuring, quality of knowledge resources, the business processes within which the lawyers are working, and so on. They sit at the intersection point between "pure business" (the lawyers) and "pure technology" (the IT team). They exhibit an ambidextrous ability to work within – and most importantly bridge across – those two worlds. This is a critical underpinning for any "innovation" work with a firm or department.

Operationally, often knowledge management leaders take their understanding of the legal practice and manage the distillation of that knowledge into templates, which they then use to automate the production of documents or sets of documents. Or else they are asked to help do something similar at the firm level by organizing "what we know" in some form of internally facing portal (or some form of "enterprise" search application). Either, or both, of these approaches take a KM leader into unfamiliar territory, requiring them to work with new technology (document automation or intranet/portals). This starts them down the slippery and uneven path towards legal innovation.

Whether it is document automation or portals of some sort, the KM professional is required to not just incrementally improve what lawyers are doing, but now to be fundamentally changing how they work. With document automation, it is replacing some of the work of the lawyers (or paralegals); with portals/intranet, replacing "does anyone know" emails/conversations with on-screen assistance. Both of these scenarios require the KM team to understand the context for the work, the culture surrounding the work, and the business objectives of the firm (or practice group).

This change, while appearing perhaps to be incremental, is actually a profound shift towards the world of "innovation".

Looking at this using an "operational" lens, both KM projects (beyond templates) and "innovative" projects use the same organizational "muscles" to be successful. These muscles include the ability to see and work across multiple dimensions at the same time. Some of those dimensions are:

- Business operations/business cases;
- Culture/leadership;
- Software implementations/configuration;
- Communication/change management;
- Political decision-making within the firm; and
- Metadata/data structure/cybersecurity.

The consequence is that there is a tendency, often recognized by firm/department leadership, that if you are good at KM projects then you will likely be good at "innovation" projects.

These types of KM projects now move you into the "change management" perspective. The further the organization moves from the incremental change to existing practices and processes, the more challenging it becomes to drive the behavioral change required to deliver on the expected business results. Here too we see where the KM function is well suited to morph into the "innovation" one. At the core of all knowledge management work is the idea that someone needs to "know" something different – and to act on it, or, at the very least, to seek knowledge in a different way (e.g., online catalogue versus going to the law library).

So, inherent in KM is the idea that you need to entice a set of independent actors (in the case of lawyers, typically, very independent ones!) to do something different. It is reasonable to contrast this with other organizational change efforts that are usually both much more prescriptive and less directly involved with the doing of the actual professional work (e.g., "to get your expenses paid, you must submit your data using the new expenses system"). Successful knowledge managers are thus well lined up to take on "innovation".

Gaps

We have seen how, underpinned by the fundamental logic of organizations engaged in the application of expert knowledge – and across three different perspectives (the tactical, the operational, and the "change management") – the work of KM is aligned with the work of "innovation" within legal organizations.

There are some gaps, however, that make this relationship more akin to a fraternal twin rather than an identical one. First, innovation work requires a mechanism or process for both the generation of ideas (ideation) along with the ability to choose the "best" ideas for investment (if only to proof-of-concept stage). There are many different mechanisms for this kind of work (e.g., business challenges, online "innovation" social platforms, stage-gating) and this would be new ground for most KM teams.

Second, KM work tends to focus on incremental improvement within an existing business model. Innovation work often pushes you further, ultimately towards business model invention (or reinvention). This requires innovation teams to understand not just the "business", but also the model(s) underlying the business – and the alternatives or options for the business. The question most KM teams start with is, "How can we help the lawyers be more efficient?", whereas innovation teams might ask, "How can we reinvent this work or create entirely new services?".

This leads to the third critical difference – the nature and kind of change management required (including stakeholder management) is at an order-of-magnitude higher for those engaged in true innovation. It is worth quoting the greatest change manager ever – Niccolò Machiavelli – from almost five hundred years ago:

> *"There is nothing more difficult to take in hand, more perilous to conduct, or more uncertain in its success, than to take the lead in the introduction of a new order of things. Because the innovator has for enemies all those who have done well under the old conditions, and lukewarm defenders in those who may do well under the new. This coolness arises partly from fear of the opponents, who have the laws on their side, and partly from the incredulity of men, who do not readily believe in new things until they have had a long experience of them. Thus, it happens that whenever those who are hostile have the opportunity to attack they do it like partisans, whilst the others defend lukewarmly."*[2]

New order of things

Those engaged in "innovation" are truly working to introduce a "new order of things"; as a result they will receive only lukewarm support while facing hostility from those who feel the uncertainty of change combined with those who feel their status threatened. This combination – of threatened status and uncertainty – along with restrictions on autonomy is the source of much of the resistance to most efforts in legal organizations to change. David Rock's neuroscience-based SCARF model (Status, Certainty, Autonomy, Relatedness, Fairness) elucidates the underlying psychological mechanisms underpinning this resistance.[3] Lawyers are especially focused on their Status, on precedent (giving them Certainty), and Autonomy (drilled into them from law school onwards as part of their professional ethics).

In truth, there is no hard and fast line between "KM" and "innovation" projects. As we have seen, "KM" underpins all the work within a professional service-based organization. As the KM work shifts from redistributing knowledge to restructuring the knowledge work, or creating new knowledge, teams begin to enter the innovation realm.

So, these two streams of work – KM and innovation – truly are fraternal twins separated at birth but inextricably intertwined by both nature and nurture. The challenge for KM teams and leaders, if they wish to be successful in this activity called "innovation", is to transcend their initial starting premise of treating knowledge as a "thing" to be moved or corralled. Instead, they have to see that knowledge is really a flow built into the warp and weave of the firm or department itself. It is embedded in the business processes and it underpins the very business logic upon which the entire organization is based.

References

1 shorturl.at/fDJQZ
2 Niccolò Machiavelli, *The Prince*, 1532, Chapter VI.
3 David Rock, "SCARF: a brain-based model for collaborating with and influencing others," *NeuroLeadership Journal*, Issue one, 2008, https://web.archive.org/web/20100705024057/http://www.your-brain-at-work.com/files/NLJ_SCARFUS.pdf.

Chapter 11:
Hybrid competitive intelligence – gathering intel remotely

By Mark Gediman, senior research analyst, Alston & Bird, LLP, and Kevin Miles, manager, research services, Norton Rose Fulbright

We all remember where we were when the work environment changed. For us, it was 13 March 2020. We were sitting at our desks when we got the word that our offices would be closed due to exploding COVID-19 infection numbers. At the time, we had no idea how providing virtual services to a virtual firm was going to work. Home challenges also required a major adjustment. Whether it was jostling for network space with the other members of our family (who were also stuck at home) or making sure the dog was able to go out (and come in and go out and come in…), it all required adapting to a new normal. Which, we're pleased to report, we did. This probably isn't new to anyone reading this. Now, on the other side of the pandemic, we have a hybrid remote/in-person work environment that requires still more adjustments. One major change is how Competitive Intelligence (CI) was conducted during this shift. This chapter discusses different aspects of these changes, from the cultural shifts in our workplaces to the ethics involved in hybrid CI.

Transitioning to a hybrid environment – cultural shifts

The pandemic changed our lives and how we conduct business changed with it. On a personal level, who would have thought that home grocery delivery would be a permanent feature, restaurants would have curb-side service and food delivery, or masks would be required?

On a professional level, these changes in our lives have affected the way we conduct business. Many CI professionals now work from home, conduct meetings virtually, and rely more on online resources than before. There are various models of professional CI work that incorporate these adjustments.

Before the pandemic, competitive intelligence professionals worked in the office five days a week. As we entered the pandemic, we worked from home.

Exiting the pandemic, we are transitioning again. Professional firms are struggling to find a happy medium between days spent working remotely and in the office. Should partners be in the office five days a week? Should office services be in four days a week on a staggered basis? Should CI professionals be allowed to work from home five days a week, with the option to work from the office one day a week or month?

The transition model used depends on the culture of the law firm. Every day we see a new report about how one firm mandates employees to work from the office two days a week and another firm mandates five days a week. This creates a recruiting opportunity when attorneys perceive the "grass is greener on the other side".

Table 1: Transition models in workplaces.

Pre-pandemic	Pandemic	Post-pandemic	Future?
Work from office 40 hours a week	Work from home 50 hours a week	Hybrid office/home – two or three days a week either home or office	Hybrid home/office – one or two days a month in the office
Work travel full-time one to two hours each way	No work travel	Weekly work – travels part-time	Very reduced work travel to no travel
Print resources 80 percent, online resources 20 percent	Flip. Online resources 80 percent, print resources 20 percent	Online resources 90 percent, print resources ten percent	Online resources 95 percent, print resources five percent
Face-to-face meetings, 100 percent	Virtual meetings, 100 percent	Hybrid meetings 60 percent virtual, 40 percent face-to-face	Hybrid meetings 80 percent virtual, 20 percent face-to-face

Source: Miles, Kevin: "Hybrid survey of private Texas Law Librarians", June 2022.

Strengths and opportunities

For CI professionals, the shifts in culture have created new strengths and opportunities. CI professionals now have a chair at the virtual table. The reports we provide attorneys have specific purposes. For litigators, CI professionals find detailed litigation information such as the number of law firms representing a particular client, judicial biographies, motion analysis, and the time from file to trial. For corporate practice, CI professionals report on a corporation's subsidiaries, the names and contact information of the general counsel, officers and directors, and merger and acquisition analysis. For the trademark practice group, a survey of royalty rates for a target company, and an analysis of the target company's trademarks.

Table 2: Overview of strengths and opportunities.

Strengths	Opportunities
Market strategy	Present an overview of shrinking and expanding markets. Describe what is causing each one in your market. How do we get from here to there?
Business research	What new activities are happening in your immediate market? You can monitor resources to discover who is moving into your market. Graph the statistics that suggest new trends. Develop a SWOT (Strengths, Weaknesses, Opportunities, and Threats) analysis on an existing client.
Cross-selling	Where is the pandemic hitting your firm? Health Insurance Portability and Accountability Act (HIPAA) (Pub.L. 104–191), Occupational Safety and Health Administration (OSHA), insurance, data breaches, and supply chain issues are affecting many clients. Other areas include food security or food technology, fintech, and IT services. You can help the firm craft a plan to cross-sell new services to existing clients.
Article writing	Your skills at writing can place firm stories in the legal press. Mapping regulations tables, writing client alerts, and writing great proposals are some of the documents you can create.

Managing expectations in a hybrid environment

Like most law firm employees in this hybrid environment, we are sitting at our desks in our home offices working on complex research projects when an email with the dreaded red exclamation point (!) hits our inbox. Immediately we open it and read the contents:

"I need a complete briefing on XYZ Inc in one hour for a lunch meeting. Please let me know this has been received and you're working on this."

One hour?! One hour usually means sending what we call a "Tear sheet". This format typically contains basic information on the company and, for a lunch meeting, basic information about the person the attorney is meeting with and the topic of the pitch.

The reference interview is essential for this type of request, regardless of the deliverable timeframe. At this point, take a moment to jot down four questions for the information necessary to adequately research this report:

1. Who is the attorney meeting with?
2. What type of work is being pitched? i.e., employment litigation, environmental remediation advice, transactional.
3. What information is most important for this meeting?
4. Taking the time constraints into account, is the attorney aware of the type of product to be delivered?

From the home office, we pick up the phone and place a call (the most efficient method of communication due to the time constraints) and ask the questions listed above. By discussing needs and report limitations upfront, this communicates to the attorney that (a) the researcher has received the request, (b) understands the request, and (c) made the attorney aware of what they can expect for the deliverable. This process goes a long way in managing expectations.

Managing the requestor's expectations is a key component of the successful competitive intelligence operation. Frustration by attorneys with delivery times and formats could cause the CI service to fail. Therefore, it's important for the consumers of the information to clearly understand the direct relationship between turnaround time, purpose, and the format of the deliverable reports.

As shown in the previous example, the depth, type, and quality of the report is directly affected by when it is due. The following tables provide an overview of the various scenarios, and the attorney should be aware of each one at the start of the project.

Table 3: Reports by time constraint.[1]

Turnaround time	Deliverable	Contents
Short term (about one hour)	Tear sheet or Data dump – no analyst analysis	Prepackaged reports* Recent news Directory information
Same day	Email or short memo – minimal analysis with high-level conclusions	Prepackaged reports* Short in-house memorandum covering predefined limited information Curated news
Long-term (three to seven days)	Briefing pack Key analysis and findings summarized by the analyst	Detailed, in-depth report Graphs and charts where appropriate Analysis of legal work, both inside the firm and by other firms Important news in relation to the practice mix of the firm and the strengths of the attorney pitching the work

**Examples of prepackaged reports include but are not limited to Monitor Suite, Thomson Reuters, Lexis Context, Lex Machina, Hoovers, Trellis, or Bloomberg Law Analytics.*

The purpose for the report determines which content is included. This prevents the use of the same specific template for all requests. Simply put, different purposes call for different reports (see Table 4).

Table 4: Report by purpose.[2]

Purpose	Report format	Types of information
Lunch/dinner meeting	Tear sheet (single page)	Significant company news Current top-level financials Which firms do they use currently? Information specific to the meeting participants Previous internal contacts?
Formal pitch meeting	Detailed information and analysis	Above items PLUS: Company profile SWOT analysis
RFP Response	Detailed information and analysis	Above items PLUS: Profiles of interviewers and executives Financial analysis Company's legal challenges Scope of RFP and how the firm aligns with it
Lateral evaluation*	Detailed information and analysis	Practice mix Representative cases (if applicable) Presentations from the prospect Articles both written by and about the prospect
Internal RFPs*	Detailed information and analysis	Clients Cases filed against Principals' background check

**Supporting documents should be included in these reports for on-demand reference.*

This is not an exhaustive list. Table 4 demonstrates that different purposes require custom reports. Templates are useful for reports but locking in specific types of data can be a challenge.

Taking these tables together shows the importance of the reference interview. Each row represents a necessary data point. The turnaround time and the purpose are just as important as the research subject. These tables do not stand alone. It's necessary to know what the categories are from both tables to produce the right product for the circumstances.

We were able to knock out the request, put it in an easy-to-read format and send it to the attorney in the allotted time. Now, back to our regularly scheduled research…

Use of virtual tools

Which tools do you use to build a CI report for companies? Naturally, this is a function of your firm's budget, and the region of the country where you practice. The tools below are useful and represent a sampling of commonly used tools. Virtual tools are not found in books but are categorized as online or via the internet.

Table 5: CI virtual tools.

CI virtual tool	Purposes	Vendor/publisher
Capital IQ (S&P)	Robust company information about officers, directors, and detailed facts about M&A deals.	This tool is a product of Standard & Poor's, which has a very robust collection of public and some private companies. Cap IQ allows customization of reports so they are relevant. Bios of the officers and directors are available for many companies. You can set news alerts for ESG matters.
Excel spreadsheet (Microsoft)	Pivot tables, graphs, and charts.	Each iteration of Microsoft's Excel Spreadsheet includes easier reporting because Microsoft listens to its customers. Pivot tables are now a breeze to build, and a necessary tool for every CI professional.
FactSet.com	Robust company information with strong analytics. Great for activist backgrounders.	FactSet helps CI professionals who need to do specific investment research, track ESG developments, or report about specific markets. One of the tools is supply chain relationships, another is understanding activist campaigns.
Hoovers/D&B (D&B)	Similar to Capital IQ, but the Hoovers reports have more international materials.	Hoovers, owned by D&B, is great for insights about US and global companies. Sometimes, this is the only source that provides company information that is not available elsewhere.
Intelligize (Lexis)	Intelligize has deep dives with SEC documents, with more analytics for reports.	Intelligize is a Lexis company which offers deep dives about companies. When a current SEC document "incorporates by reference," a few clicks bring those older items forward. This saves a lot of time and effort. Lately, Intelligize has increased the visual analytics of company reports.
Monitor Suite (Thomson Reuters)	Monitor Suite presents a lot of material with current information.	Thomson Reuters has developed Monitor Suite into a strong product for monitoring litigation and deals. CI professionals find this an easy platform to maneouvre. The reports are very accurate and influential.

continued on next page

CI virtual tool	Purposes	Vendor/publisher
Pitchbook.com	Private company reports with strong emphasis about investment companies.	Pitchbook is great for information about private equity, mergers and acquisitions and venture capital. The information is well-organized and easy to find. Moreover, Pitchbook has a Chrome extension, Excel plugin, and Application Programing Interfaces (APIs) for increasing report flexibility.
SEC.gov (US Securities and Exchange Commission)	A government agency, the SEC has reorganized information with expandable panels about the company and gathering 10-K reports in a findable place.	The US Securities and Exchange Commission is free. Recent improvements include three panels that save the time of the CI professional. First, Company Information expands to reveal the CIK, EIN, SIC, state location, state of incorporation, business address and phone number, any former names, and the number of filings to date. Second, the Latest Filings panel reveals the latest five filings, which can be expanded to show more. Third, Selected Filings group reports by 8-K, 10-K, Proxy, and Ownership disclosures.
Virtual Litigation Analytics Tools		
Bloomberg Law	Bloomberg Law has a strong litigation analytics platform that provides analytics on attorneys, judges, companies, law firms, and courts.	Bloomberg Law further divides the information into these categories for company information: law firm, attorney, case type, jurisdiction and litigation history.
Lexis Context	Lexis Context is great for an overview, analytics of motions and citation patterns, and documents.	Lexis Context provides overviews of state and federal judges, experts, attorneys, and companies with analytics for motion language, citation patterns, outcomes, and documents. One can link to Lexis Context from Courtlink.
Lex Machina	Lex Machina continually expands its coverage beyond intellectual property to additional nature of suit with many ways to rearrange report formats.	Lex Machina is a Lexis product that has great information organized by court and by type for federal district court cases. Additionally, Lex Machina has a Quick Tools platform with nine sections: courts and judges comparator, law firms comparator, parties comparator, motion kick starter, attorney team analyzer, early case assessor, patent portfolio litigation evaluator, expert witness explorer, and COVID-19 impact analyzer.
Trellis	Trellis is expanding beyond California to other large legal markets. It provides great intel for cases at the state level.	Great for state court filings, Trellis has judge research, legal research, motion research, and opposing counsel research. Verdicts were recently added.

There are some drawbacks to using open-source collaboration tools. CI reports often contain confidential and proprietary data that should not be shared outside of the organization. Use of third-party virtual drives may be prohibited by firm policy, and may not be secure. It is better to use internal collaboration tools such as Teams, Slack, Jabber, and Zoom that keep the documents and data inside the organization's network. Maintaining data security is paramount for competitive intelligence professionals.

Ethics and CI are not mutually exclusive

No matter the working environment, ethics are essential to the reputation and success of every CI professional. Reliability and trustworthiness directly relate to the value they bring to the table. An "end justifies the means" attitude undermines the acceptance of the professional's work product. This applies to conversations with others outside the firm as well as online research.

Why are ethics so important? Here are two reasons:

1. *Trust.* The CI professional obtains information, analyzes it, and presents it to the firm. If the CI professional's character is suspect in any way, their work product would be equally tainted. Falsely identifying oneself on a phone call or in an email could give the researcher an untrustworthy reputation both internally and externally. A firm takes strategic action based on the quality of the CI professional's research and analysis, as well as their sterling reputation. The researcher's work product must be above reproach.
2. *Liability.* Information obtained under false pretenses can result in penalties to the firm, including, but not limited to, embarrassment, sanctions, loss of client, and loss of reputation for both the firm and the researcher; grounds for termination for the CI professional, who will certainly have difficulty finding another position; and possible criminal penalties resulting from the misrepresentation.

Here's a sample exchange showing the application of ethics in research and communication:

> The phone is ringing at the desk in the (home) office. An official from an agency the researcher emailed a document request to the day before is on the line. After the introductions, she has the following conversation:

OFFICIAL: "I'm sorry, but I need to ask this: Can you tell me who your client is?"

RESEARCHER: "Sorry, the attorney hasn't shared that information with me. I don't even have a billing number for this project."

OFFICIAL: "Okay, well, we're short-staffed and I wanted to make sure we haven't already provided these documents. I can get these to you in about a day or so."

RESEARCHER: "Thank you very much! I appreciate your help."

In the researcher's prior email, she identified herself and her firm. She was very clear that she was a law firm librarian conducting research for an unspecified attorney.

This conversation is an example of ethical communication. The researcher identified herself and her firm affiliation in her email. She made it very clear from both her written and verbal communications that there was information she could and could not provide, and she gave reasons for the latter. There may be information you are not able to provide for a variety of reasons. If you can't tell the person who your employer is, say so. Don't make something up. If they choose to end the conversation at that point, so be it.

When gathering CI information ethically, keep the following points in mind:

1. Do not misrepresent yourself. If you cannot answer a question, say so and, if you are able to, give an honest reason for why you can't. In our experience, this doesn't often result in the end of the conversation.
2. Do not make up data or information, especially if you think it will tell a story the requestor wants to hear.
3. A corollary of (2): include the bad with the good in your reports. An honest and balanced analysis of the issue and the prospective client/competitor is what the attorney needs to hear, even though it may not be what they want to hear.

This advice may sound trite but behaving unethically is not worth the consequences.

Summing up

As researchers, CI professionals are not exempt from the need to continually adapt to the changing cultural demands and evolving research landscape of the post-pandemic workplace. Some traditional tools, such as SWOT analysis, are still important to provide a detailed picture of the value an organization can bring to a prospective client. Ethics are especially relevant when research is conducted remotely by phone and email. The hybrid workspace is not a hinderance to in-depth research and detailed analyses.

References

1 Adapted from Gediman, Mark, "Managing Expectations in the Age of Working from Home," AALL Spectrum, November/December 2020, pp. 40-41.

2 *Ibid.*

Chapter 12:
Retaining KM talent

By Tara Pichardo-Angadi, head of knowledge (EMEA), Norton Rose Fulbright LLP

Introduction

Law firms have learned many lessons during the pandemic and have had to adapt quickly to new ways of working. For those that invested in knowledge in prior years, this was the time to reap the benefits of their strategy. Whether it was through subject matter experts, able to analyze the complex and rapidly changing situation and produce thought leadership, or through communities of practice, stepping up to create virtual teams and share knowledge using the latest technology, this global challenge has shown the importance of knowledge management. However, as has been noted in all sectors and regions, we are also now faced with what has been labelled the "great resignation", as workers reassess their options and seek more flexibility, greater purpose, or higher compensation. The war on talent is real, and those leading knowledge management professionals know this only too well.

So, how can you ensure you are retaining your KM talent?

It all starts with hiring, which in this competitive market is tricky and takes both time and effort.

Hiring

- What is your employer KM brand?
- What is your USP in hiring KM talent?
- How can you differentiate from your competitors?
- How do you ensure you can find untapped talent?
- Importance of onboarding

Of course, it is important to get compensation right, for example through benchmarking roles, to ensure you are able to compete in the market for

KM talent. However, compensation alone will not necessarily allow you to hire and much less retain top talent. In this post-pandemic age, people are less likely to be motivated by compensation alone – their expectations include having a sense of purpose and the ability to do what they truly love (see more on this below).

How do you define your employer brand when it comes to KM professionals? How does the legal KM community view the law firm? What might your unique selling proposition be when it comes to hiring KM talent? These are the sorts of questions you should be asking as you prepare to brief your recruitment advisers. Your KM team will be best placed to help you understand what the employer's brand might be and getting their input will serve the additional purpose of improving engagement within the team.

You will most likely face potential recruits who are comparing a few offers, so it is also important for you to assess your competitors. Who are they? What are they known for in the market? This will help you hone your own brand definition to ensure you are differentiating your proposition and can articulate this to candidates.

One change, which is ostensibly here for good, is the ability to work remotely. Some form of flexible and remote working is now a requisite for most recruits. We may find ourselves having to go even further, allowing fully remote working for knowledge professionals. This will allow us to tap into new pools of talent, based in locations where the employer does not have a workplace. This may not work for roles that support business teams directly, but could more easily work for those roles with less face-to-face interaction that rely more on technology, such as knowledge systems, research, or document automation roles. Exploring this extended talent pool could help solve the shortage of experts who are in high demand.

Recently, interviews for knowledge roles have felt more like the recruiter is being interviewed than the traditional reverse. Interviewees have a better sense of what they want from a new role and what they expect from an employer. It makes sense, given that candidates often only have a few meetings during which to decide between prospective employers. Of course, firms should think carefully about who should be trusted as an ambassador for the employer brand. Inviting a number of key people to the interview will show the applicant the firm's commitment to the role. It will also allow candidates to get a view of the diverse make-up of their potential new stakeholders.

Firms will need to show greater agility when it comes to measuring their KM needs and ensuring the perfect fit in a new recruit. Increasingly, employers have to draw from a much wider talent pool, including profiles they might have overlooked previously. It is important to keep an open mind when recruiting for KM roles and this might mean hiring on someone's potential rather than proven records of accomplishment.

You should plan the onboarding ahead of time, to ensure your new KM talent gets the best possible first impression of the firm. Identify all those colleagues, stakeholders, and others who will allow your new joiner to make a success of their new mandate. You might want to draw up such a list and then schedule introductions over the course of a few weeks so as not to overwhelm your new KM professional. Of course, any training on tools, processes, and systems should be scheduled early on, but you could also spread the training out enough to allow your new recruit time to apply their new knowledge immediately after they have been trained. Ideally, you would plan the onboarding with a few tasks to be carried out to encourage experiential learning.

Your starry-eyed new recruit is about to join you. Congratulations! Now the real work can start.

Developing

- Impact of team structure: whom is KM reporting to?
- Importance of regular one-to-ones
- How can you help KM talent build their network?
- Creating a culture of open feedback
- What training is available to KM talent?

Once you have recruited your new KM talent it is important to retain them by understanding their top priorities. This means ensuring not only that they feel they are adequately compensated but that they are engaged and feel valued within the organization. One key way of ensuring that the talent is engaged and appreciated is to develop their skills.

One area when looking at employee engagement is to consider how your KM team is structured. In many law firms, knowledge professionals tend to fall into two categories – lawyers (professional support lawyers, knowledge management lawyers, knowledge partners and so forth; let's call them knowledge lawyers) and systems or process managers (knowledge managers, document automation specialists, product owners of relevant legal technology and the like). Whereas the latter category tends to sit in a discrete group of central knowledge management support, the former usually sit within the practice areas, sector groups, and teams they support as subject matter experts.

Some form of consistency in team structures can be beneficial, as it will allow better coordination of projects that span several practice areas and offices. If reporting lines are solely within the practice area, it may not be as easy for a knowledge lawyer to prioritize firm-wide and strategic knowledge projects. It is therefore useful for the knowledge lawyer to have a reporting line into a dedicated knowledge team leader with oversight on the firm-wide knowledge plan, who will also be able to guide new lawyers transitioning away from fee earning. The knowledge team leader will be better placed to help the new joiner build up a network of relevant colleagues across the firm, based on areas of expertise and interest, and to understand the priorities for the organization. All this will help ensure a more successful integration and lead to job satisfaction.

Much has been said, especially after the long period of enforced working from home, about the importance of regular one-to-ones with direct reports.[1] This will also be important where employees are working remotely or in hybrid mode. Regular face-to-face meetings are crucial in ensuring team members feel connected and valued. It also allows for important conversations heading off issues that could escalate if not addressed swiftly. It will allow the manager to get a sense of when someone might be feeling frustrated and at risk of resigning. Finally, it is a good way of ensuring progress is made on projects with no hard deadlines, which risk being pushed back indefinitely in the face of the daily emergencies that tend to arise. This in turn helps knowledge professionals be more productive, thereby increasing their job satisfaction. Of course, this only works if managers actually ensure that regular meetings take place. It is all too easy to cancel these meetings, seeing them as non-crucial and an easy way to regain some time. This is a tendency to be avoided if managers want to make their team members feel valued.

Building a community and a strong network in an organization is important to ensure connection. Those employees who have developed a strong network in their firm will have a harder time resigning. This is true of all companies and roles, but it is perhaps even more important for a knowledge professional. Knowledge lawyers build relationships easily within the team they support, or at least they did when people still met regularly in the office. This now requires a bit more of a conscious effort to achieve, but firms are getting there with team days in the office ("the office is the new off-site" was a phrase coined in a recent McKinsey on Talent podcast).[2]

Expanding beyond the team they support, the most successful knowledge professionals have wide and deep networks within their firms. They may have acquired this network through sheer longevity, but networks can also be created much more quickly. When a knowledge lawyer becomes known as a subject matter expert in their field, this network can grow exponentially. A team leader or partner in charge of a knowledge lawyer can help by actively seeking out opportunities for cross-pollination, even though this may take some time away from the core needs of the team the lawyer supports. Ultimately, a knowledge lawyer who has a broad network in the firm will get involved in the most interesting projects and be happier in their current role. They will also develop strong sponsors within other teams, making role changes easier, as will be discussed in the next section. In addition, the network also requires softer interactions, outside of transactional needs. A lack of social and community type activities is strongly affecting the loyalty of employees who need more in the way of day-to-day interaction with their colleagues. It's these coffee catch-ups and team events that people missed most during the pandemic and that should resume to provide the glue in building teams.

Feedback and communication is incredibly important in ensuring people develop throughout their career. We all know it, yet do not always take the time to give or ask for feedback. For a knowledge professional, feedback is even more crucial as they should keep a "client service" mindset and need to know how they are doing for their particular practice areas where one size may not fit all. Knowledge professionals will want feedback on whether the advice or training being given is clear enough and what else is needed to provide best-in-class knowledge services. This feedback should also lead to discussions around what skills the knowledge professional could continue to develop to ensure their own professional growth. Giving regular feedback to the knowledge professionals you work with will lead to better service in the future – and by showing you care about a person's development enough to take the time to give the feedback, you will ensure they feel valued and appreciated, leading to higher rates of retention. This works better when the firm has created a culture of open two-way feedback and, in particular, it will be important for knowledge professionals to be able to give feedback concerning the partners and others they support. This two-way conversation tells your knowledge team that they are considered equals in the organization, especially if you ask both fee-earning and knowledge lawyers in the team to feed into partner reviews.

Finally, give some thought to the formal learning and development opportunities that exist within your firm for knowledge professionals. They spend a lot of time training the teams they support, but who trains them? We know there is a correlation between high levels of learning and development activities and retention of employees, as can be seen in recent reports showing career development as the first factor for retaining young lawyers.[3] This also fits in with research carried out across all sectors showing that about half of what people earn during their lifetime is associated with the skills they gain through work.[4] In this, knowledge professionals are no exception. Ensure you have cross-departmental training available on legal topics, which may be of interest to all knowledge lawyers. Send your knowledge lawyers to external training in their area of expertise, so they can learn from peers and disseminate the knowledge internally. Think about other training opportunities that may be relevant to them, such as associate or partner business skills courses you run. If your firm runs annual or other performance reviews, make sure to discuss learning and development plans with your knowledge professionals to show you are committed to their growth.

Sometimes, despite having followed all the best practices set out above, your knowledge professional will nevertheless get itchy feet. It is important to spot this ahead of a resignation, as there is a lot you can do to ensure you retain top talent or help people move on gracefully.

Moving

- Importance of regular career discussions
- Importance of a career structure for KM
- Breaking down silos between teams
- How to foster a culture of loving what you do and doing what you love
- How to let go and create ambassadors

How often should you discuss career aspirations with your knowledge professionals? You could stick to the annual performance review, but the best team leaders have a more regular conversation with team members, making it easier for people to raise needs and frustrations as they arise, rather than after they've reached a decision to leave. This could be one of the recurring agenda items for your one-to-ones. It is also a good idea to foster a culture of openness in expressing career aspirations and to make it clear to your team they should come to you if they ever consider leaving, so you can help align the opportunities within your firm and try to retain them.

For a long time, knowledge professionals had very few prospects of career progression, which understandably led to frustration and meant the profession was less appealing to the more ambitious of lawyers. Most firms now offer various levels of seniority within the knowledge lawyer career – counsel, directors, sometimes even partners – although in most firms, partners move into knowledge roles rather than knowledge lawyers being promoted to the partnership. A formalized and transparent promotion track is now market standard and those firms wanting to retain their KM talent should think about what more they could do, including a partner track for their most highly regarded knowledge lawyers.

As explained in more detail above, a broad and deep network, across all areas of the firm, will lead to greater opportunities for knowledge lawyers. By broadening out and taking on projects spanning several practice areas or teams, knowledge lawyers will effectively contribute to the breaking down of silos, which many law firms struggle with. This is true for fee-earning teams (branching out into sectors covering various practice areas for example) and for business services teams (encompassing innovation, marketing, and business development, learning and development teams, and projects). Knowledge professionals thereby act as conduits between different teams, ensuring information about areas of common interest is shared. They are also useful ambassadors for firm initiatives within their teams as they will often know more about these and will be able to relay them to the fee-earners who focus on their day-to-day client-facing work. The effect of this branching out will be to develop well-rounded knowledge professionals, capable of taking on firm-wide projects and sometimes moving into other teams if they find an area to be more appealing. This is occurring in a number of organizations, which are providing their employees with cycles of experience. These opportunities to work with other teams and areas allow employees to share their own skills but also to develop new skills that they can use when they return to their day job.

One of the main challenges in talent retention since the pandemic seems to be people needing to find greater purpose in what they do. How can we create a culture where people do what they love and love what they do? In this, the knowledge community is possibly at an advantage. Knowledge lawyers make a conscious decision to take a sidestep from the traditional lawyer career path when they move into knowledge roles. This generally indicates that knowledge lawyers move to find greater purpose than they felt in traditional fee-earning roles. They may have made the move because they wanted to have more time to expand their knowledge of their area of expertise, indicating a true love of the law. They may have wanted greater insight into what was happening outside their area of practice in a broader practice-wide or sector role, indicating a passion for an industry or area of business. Whatever the reasons for the initial move into the knowledge role, matters may well have changed for them since then. As employees are more enlightened and empowered, the employer needs to be adaptable to ensure that employees are fulfilled. Employers need to ask: Do they still enjoy what they are doing? How can they be more satisfied in their day-to-day work? What truly makes them happy at work? How can they seek more of that type of work? These are all questions that managers should be raising during one-to-ones with their knowledge team.

Sometimes it simply is not possible to keep people happy in their roles and you will need to help them find other opportunities. Of course, you may find that, with their expanded network, they have already thought of other internal opportunities, or you could help them find these with your own contacts. Personally, I have always encouraged people to move from my team into other areas, as this ensures we keep talent within the firm when they want to move on. It also gives me a network of knowledge ambassadors and people I know will help spread the good word. You could even go so far as to help your people find opportunities elsewhere using your external contacts. It will expand your network of firm ambassadors in the market and help build a strong alumni group. Who knows, your former knowledge colleagues might even appreciate what you have done so much that they return to you if they find that the grass is not greener.

Conclusion

Throughout the employee lifecycle, there are steps there can be taken to seek to retain knowledge talent. This requires time and attention, but with some simple rules of communication, you will find it easier to stay ahead of the game.

References

1 See, for example, Shelley Flett, *The Dynamic Leader: Become the leader others are inspired to follow,* Major Street Publishing, 2019.

2 www.mckinsey.com/business-functions/people-and-organizational-performance/our-insights/culture-in-the-hybrid-workplace

3 See, for example, Sophie Gould, "Here comes the Next-Gen: Flex Legal's Future Lawyers Report", *Flex Legal*, 2022, https://flex.legal/blog/here-comes-the-next-gen-flex-legals-future-lawyers-report.

4 See, for example, Anu Madgavkar, Bill Schaninger, Sven Smit, Jonathan Woetzel, Hamid Samandari, Davis Carlin, Jeongmin Seong, and Kanmani Chockalingam,

"Human capital at work: The value of experience", McKinsey & Company, 2022, www.mckinsey.com/business-functions/people-and-organizational-performance/our-insights/human-capital-at-work-the-value-of-experience?.

Chapter 13:

Inclusion and diversity in knowledge: raising awareness and embedding best practice post-COVID

By Orla Bingham, service owner, content development, and Katherine Lang, senior knowledge lawyer and London knowledge lead, Baker McKenzie

Inclusion and diversity (I&D) is now an active global conversation, advancing and evolving by the day, and aspirations around enabling a wider talent pool, improving access to all and eliminating inequality are more important than ever. As a firm, Baker McKenzie proudly declares #WeAreNotNeutral, and significant inclusion and diversity initiatives take place across the firm on a global scale, which seek to embed I&D considerations in the work of our colleagues and clients.

Within Knowledge, pre-COVID was already a period of change, as we worked to better integrate our team across our international offices and within our centers in Belfast, Tampa, Buenos Aires, and Manila. As with the rest of the firm, our focus grew on developing a "one team" mentality, cohesive culture, and embedding best practice amongst our diverse knowledge team.

In 2021, our global knowledge director took a direct step to foster inclusion and celebrate diversity globally amongst the knowledge team by asking for volunteers to establish a global I&D in Knowledge Working Group. Enthusiastic team members from Amsterdam, Buenos Aires, Belfast, London, and Sydney came together to form the group, of which we are members, and which now meets quarterly.

The working group, chaired by the global knowledge director, soon identified key areas of focus that were particularly able to be delivered by a knowledge function, were personal areas of interest, or which responded to an evident need within the firm or the knowledge team. Members of the group allocated themselves to these focus areas and began to address them. This chapter sets out some of our key initiatives and learnings so far.

Inclusive training

A key part of many roles within knowledge is the delivery of legal training. The ability to deliver complex information in a digestible and memorable format to a diverse audience is a key skill. Traditionally, we might have adapted in-person training to our audience depending on its experience, understanding of the topic, or the kind of client involved. Now, however, we suggest that a much more sophisticated and multi-faceted approach is needed.

In March 2020, training moved online overnight, and the need for regular training was only heightened as a result of business disruption and a plethora of governmental policy intervention. Knowledge teams had to adapt quickly. How could we make sure our clients were updated in this fast evolving new world? How would busy people learn best when confined to working from home? We all had to learn on the job. We immediately found that simple steps could help; for example, asking participants to turn on their cameras during training, and organizing online "drop-in" sessions for colleagues to discuss queries in an informal way.

However, arguably the biggest hurdle arose when some colleagues and clients returned to the office, whilst others continued to work remotely. Training needs diversified further, with some people eager to return to in-person training, and others keen to retain the ease of online sessions. At Baker McKenzie, we introduced hybrid training sessions, and quickly realized we had a lot more to learn. Importantly, the working group recognized these hurdles as opportunities to foster inclusion, ensuring that hybrid training is inclusive and accessible to all colleagues and clients. These are some of our key takeaways from this first year of hybrid training:

- We worked with the learning and development and I&D teams to pull together the most effective ideas for hybrid training from across the business. For example, the trainer should initiate camera view for themselves and all attendees as soon as entering the "room" to immediately create a more open online environment.
- Using polls, surveys, and breakout rooms can optimize engagement and encourage group discussions amongst all members of the session, and may also be more inclusive of a range of learning styles.
- Ideally, all in-person attendees should bring their laptop to allow remote attendees to have an individual camera view of all participants. The training facilitator should be aware of, and look for, hints that remote participants would like to contribute, appreciating there is a diverse range of cultural approaches in this regard. Some people may speak directly to the room or "raise a hand", but others might turn on their video, come off mute, or simply sit up straighter when they wish

to make a contribution. Others might feel more comfortable adding their thoughts via the "chat" function, which should be monitored during the session.

- For some people with a disability, the increase in online training during the pandemic was very welcome, being more accessible in many ways. For example, hearing aid users might connect to a remote session using Bluetooth, and enable closed-captioning, which is more inclusive than a traditional training session. We should, however, be aware that hybrid training can also present challenges for participants and trainers with a disability, whether that is accessing the training room, or monitoring contributions from both the in-person attendees and those online.
- Similar consideration should be given to language differences. In a global context, training may not be delivered in a participant's first language. It is vital to make sure training is delivered in an appropriate way, with language and visual aids being clear and comprehensible, bearing in mind it may be easier to read what is being said on screen as well as simply listening.

The knowledge function at Baker McKenzie distributes a regular newsletter, "In the Know", which serves as a regular update and method of communication with the entire global team. The working group has leveraged the wide reach of the newsletter to promote some of these points amongst the global knowledge community.

Inclusive language

Inclusive language has come to the fore in recent years, with heightened awareness of the use of language or references that could offend, alienate, or exclude people on the basis of gender identity and expression. This risk is increased in an international, multi-lingual environment, and particularly where colleagues have been onboarded remotely during the pandemic.

For years, the status quo, particularly in legal environments, has been to adopt the traditional "masculine" version of language in communications, documents, and policies, reinforcing the perception that most lawyers or business professionals are men. This continues to perpetuate gender bias, and may unconsciously offend or alienate people.

Adopting inclusive language has been an important step in the firm's broader I&D campaign, and in 2020, working with the global diversity and inclusion chair, the knowledge function launched its Inclusive Language

Project. The knowledge team was integral to the project, with the goal of achieving gender neutrality in the firm's standard form precedents, templates, policies, client materials and other essential content, ultimately benefiting our clients. This required a review of the existing knowledge base and the implementation of guidelines when approaching drafting exercises, moving forward.

With a global library of around 74,000 documents across 44 jurisdictions, amending existing knowhow would be no small feat, and a change of every document ever created would be impossible. The project therefore required a targeted approach, with efforts focused on the most frequently used documents in the firm's SharePoint-based knowledge repository, Harmony. Guidelines were drawn up addressing three key issues – salutations, pronouns, and gender-specific nouns. Gender-specific salutations such as "Dear Sirs" were replaced by neutral alternatives such as "Dear all" or "Dear [Company name]". Gender-specific pronouns such as "she/he" were substituted for "they", and gender assumptions in relation roles were removed, for example, the use of "chair" in place of "chairman".

In a trial exercise, the top 100 most viewed documents in the US Harmony libraries were reviewed for gender-specific language, with approximately 20 percent having some sort of gender identification issue, and the remaining documents requiring minor alteration for gender-specific pronouns. The project was therefore expanded to include review of the top 100 documents in the Australian and English precedent libraries, with a team of knowledge paralegals taking the lead, working with document owners to make changes in a sensitive way, whilst maintaining the privacy and integrity of each document itself. This is an ongoing project, which is likely to expand across all key markets, and is pivotal to Knowledge's ongoing I&D efforts. We are also incorporating our legal tech solutions to help automate the process and ultimately drive efficiency in the project.

The guidelines are now being used proactively in the firm's A-Z style guide, which sets out best practice for content generation and now includes an inclusive language check for all new content created. This has also been incorporated into onboarding procedures for new joiners within the knowledge team, embedding use of gender-neutral language in day-to-day activities and processes from the outset.

On a broader scale, colleagues within the firm are encouraged to be mindful of the use of inclusive language in daily interactions, which has been vital during a time when communications, for the large part, have been by digital means. Colleagues have been encouraged to indicate their preferred pronouns in their email footer, to enhance communications and facilitate openness within the firm. We are also now considering how we can support our clients with their efforts to adopt a more inclusive language approach across their content and communications.

Inclusion of all colleagues

Only by taking an inclusive approach to all colleagues can we make sure that everyone within our teams has an equal chance of support. There is a risk that colleagues who have joined large law firms remotely during or after the pandemic can struggle to feel part of the organizational culture.

At Baker McKenzie, we decided that an I&D buddy program across the knowledge function could provide a solution to this. We are modeling this on the successful integration mentoring program that has been implemented in some of our North American teams. This program individually matches mentors and mentees for a year, and provides detailed guidance to the pair as to how to plan and manage their mentoring relationship. The organizer of the program checks in with the pair throughout the year, both to discuss integration generally but also to provide guidance if there are any concerns with the mentoring relationship. Additionally, a budget is provided so that the mentor and mentee can meet outside of the office in a more neutral venue at no extra cost to themselves.

Allyship

Demonstrating allyship is an important step towards an inclusive workplace. This is especially important for members of a global knowledge team, who may have frequent contact with a wide range of people across the firm. Allyship is the idea that even if a person does not personally identify with an area of I&D, they can still be an active supporter of those who do. That person can use their voice to advocate for them, and understand the challenges that they face in their daily lives. A visible ally can, for example, be a powerful support to those in very small teams, or to a lone member of the knowledge team in a local office.

The working group, itself formed of allies, has started to promote allyship amongst our community. We started by publishing a piece in "In The Know" to explain allyship and suggest practical steps that our team members can take at a personal, interpersonal, and functional level:

- *Personal.* Pick an area of diversity that resonates. Join or create your office committee, sign up to an email list, or attend events/social functions.

- *Interpersonal.* Become a "buddy", mentor, or sponsor someone from an under-represented community.
- *Functional.* Invite people from diverse backgrounds to talk about their experiences in team meetings or prepare a profile on them for team newsletters. Ensure that everyone is invited to talk at meetings that you chair or attend.

The working group also invited a high-profile partner ally to present a "fireside chat" in a global knowledge community online meeting, explaining what allyship means to her and why she decided to become a visible ally. It is hoped that promoting and normalizing allyship at the most senior levels of the firm will encourage many more colleagues to follow suit.

Bringing your whole self to work

The pandemic changed daily interactions and relationships with colleagues and clients on so many levels, not least in relation to our ability to foster relationships and create a sense of "belonging" within teams. Working remotely for such an extended period has, for many, barred access to deeper or more open and honest dialogues about who they are and how they feel. The working group opened up a virtual channel to address this, promoting the concept of "bring your whole self to work" through storytelling. We identified some I&D champions and enthusiasts, inviting them to share pictures and sometimes very personal stories about their experiences with I&D in "In The Know", with one colleague nominating another in each edition.

We hope that these acts of courage and vulnerability will inspire others to take the same step, with the goal of normalizing conversations on a personal level so that colleagues can discover the whole person beyond the professional title. This also demonstrates that the team works in an environment where it is OK, and is in fact encouraged, to bring your whole self to work.

There is now also a general expectation of managers to ensure the development of personal and social connections within their teams. A segment of knowledge calls and town halls across a number of offices are now dedicated to personal updates, the subject matter being left open to the contributors, whether in relation to family, hobbies, or wider interests and lifestyles. This change has proved invaluable for keeping in touch and improving social connections amongst the team during a time when face-to-face connections have been curtailed, but has also contributed to the general perception of openness, inclusion, and of being able to bring your whole self to work.

Returning to the workplace

Returning to the "new normal" and office working post-COVID has posed challenges for us all, not least for those with particular needs or unique circumstances.

In many ways, the pandemic created a more level playing field from an I&D perspective. For example, people with caring responsibilities were more likely to avail of working from home opportunities pre-COVID, making them "less visible" and potentially limiting access to networks and opportunities. With the exception of "key workers", everyone was forced out of the workplace when COVID hit, which also mitigated some of the difficulties faced by minority groups, such as those with physical limitations, or those encountering implicit or explicit discrimination or bias. It is perhaps unsurprising, therefore, that a return to the office environment in 2022 presented numerous concerns and opportunities in the I&D space.

Within knowledge specifically, our teams often work within small groups, in global roles, or with those in other offices. Knowledge calls have nearly always taken place virtually, function-wide communications are sent out by email or other digital means, and training sessions have become confined to the virtual world. This naturally posed the question of whether being physically present in an office would be necessary going forward. However, despite the multitude of benefits of home working, it's important to bear in mind the drawbacks, not least in relation to impact on mental health, training gaps, inhibited development (particularly for more junior colleagues), and a general lack of inclusion across teams.

The post-COVID return to work presented an opportunity to adapt to the needs of the team, with the implementation of largely hybrid working structures across all offices being introduced. A general expectation was set for knowledge teams to attend the office at least part of the week, but this has been applied in an agile way to account for those with specific needs, for example, single parents requiring more home working solutions, or disabled employees with difficulties commuting to or navigating the office. Consideration was also given to those with health vulnerabilities, and empathy and understanding around the difficulties of reintegrating into the new working model were top of mind for leaders.

Across knowledge, different methods were employed to ease this reintegration, including "Staying Connected" sessions, encouraging teams to implement strategies to stay connected in the new hybrid world, including encouraging social interaction by leveraging our various technology channels, promoting regular wellbeing chats, and careful monitoring of new joiners. Teams were encouraged to establish "anchor" days to ensure in-person meetings on at least one day per week, whilst also maintaining flexibility to address individual needs. Lunch and learn sessions were set up across different offices to re-establish group networking opportunities, and adapting to conducting hybrid meetings became imperative.

Going forward, focus remains on teams retaining the flexibility to fulfil their hours and ultimately service our clients in a way that suits their needs, lifestyles and commitments, rather than being tied to the traditional nine-to-five office model, which potentially disadvantaged many.

What next?

The working group has started its work productively. Beginning in the midst of the pandemic, and consolidating its work whilst continuing to be impacted by COVID-19 has certainly been challenging. We have, however, achieved some real results – from changes to the way that training is delivered, increased use of inclusive language and proactive encouragement of gender-neutral language with new joiners, to visible, high-profile allyship, and sharing and accommodation of vulnerabilities amongst team members, in ways that would have been unheard of even a few years ago.

We now need to continue to monitor the wider I&D work within the firm, and indeed across other firms, and to take a proactive and joined-up approach, including continuing to support and share with our clients. We are increasingly considering how to leverage our various technology solutions to enable this goal – for example, using our research teams and aggregator tool, InfoNgen, to constantly surface I&D developments across the globe, tailored to the client's needs. We have also created a repository of I&D material on our legal update Insight+ platform that clients can tap into, to address I&D considerations within their own organizations.

Our work has certainly been facilitated by role modeling and the strong internal network and knowledge-sharing culture that already existed, and being able to immediately leverage "In The Know" and global knowledge community calls to promote our I&D work has been vital to our efforts. The firm's wider I&D initiatives in areas such as allyship and buddying, and wider learning and development work on inclusive meetings and training have also given us some ready-made frameworks that have been relatively easy to integrate into the knowledge context.

That isn't to say that we face no hurdles going forward. So what is next? Our team members are busy on core work and we need to keep up momentum on I&D so that it remains visible and front of mind. We need to continue to share best practice and key learnings to ensure that we continuously improve the inclusivity of the training we deliver to our teams and clients.

In this way, we hope that members of our knowledge community will continue to feel safe, accepted, included, and heard.

Chapter 14:
Building and managing a truly global research team post-COVID

By Kathy Skinner, director of research, White & Case LLP

Changes to research teams post-COVID and their impact on global team-building and alignment

The global pandemic has brought lasting changes to all aspects of our lives, including our work roles and our workplaces. This chapter provides strategies for global research teams responding to some of the resulting challenges and realizing opportunities created or hastened by the sudden move to remote and hybrid working.

Global research teams are now working under a multitude of scenarios. Some of us are navigating returning to the office on a hybrid basis, a few of us have returned full-time, and others are working fully remotely and may never return to an office. To make it more complicated, this range of scenarios may exist within a single research team in a single firm. In addition, policies continue to be in flux and many firms are reevaluating their initial decisions about hybrid work arrangements. In this chapter we'll outline some best practices for navigating those different scenarios.

Managing remote teams

Managing a remote team requires a different set of skills than managing a team in an office, and firms should be prepared to help their leaders acquire the necessary management and leadership skills to keep their teams connected and engaged in the absence of daily face-to-face contact. Not all team members will respond in the same way to remote or hybrid work, and for some team members and some roles, maintaining engagement is natural and the personal life benefits far outweigh any downsides of remote work. For others, the lack of interaction or consistent guidance, distractions at home, or lack of structure make working from home unmotivating and unproductive. Managers operating in these varied environments will have to ensure that they have the range of management and leadership skills needed, and this will likely require learning new ways of working.

The in-person interactions in an office that provided opportunities for consistent coaching and guidance need to happen in other ways in a remote environment. These new ways of working could include:

- More focused and intentional one-on-one check-ins with team members and supervisors;
- Training managers to use key performance indicators (KPIs) as a way to measure performance and productivity and to provide related coaching in the absence of the ability to observe productivity first hand;
- Standardizing research and creating a catalogue of core product offerings and templates that can be delivered consistently across the team;
- Re-establishing priorities and strategy with one-, three-, and five-year time horizons. It makes sense to consider whether there are high impact "quick wins" that you can start with, such as providing a few client-facing offerings;
- Revisiting your organizational structure to determine whether it needs to be adjusted to reflect remote working. For example, determining whether you can use this opportunity to de-silo some aspects of your function and move from local to regional or even to global roles; and
- Similarly, thinking about how remote working drives recruiting and hiring. Perhaps you have new opportunities to recruit more broadly to find the best candidates who can service multiple locations, regardless of where their "home" office is.

What are the biggest long-term challenges and what organizational support do you need to address them?

In a remote environment, in the absence of informal day-to-day interactions with team members, supervisors, and firm management, aligning around a common vision and priorities becomes even more crucial. "Managing up" and maintaining visibility and alignment are essential. How do you ensure that you and your manager are aligned and that he or she is aware of what you are focused on and is able to help as needed in a hybrid working environment? As noted above, one effective approach is to make sure to have one-on-one calls at least bi-weekly and to take time to prepare thoroughly for those calls.

Tips for impactful one-on-one meetings with your supervisor or for your direct reports

- Prepare tight but thoughtful agendas and send them the day before the call. Prioritize the most impactful items and omit items of lesser importance that you can resolve on your own.
- Use one-on-one meetings to inform your supervisor about things that may come to his or her attention in another context and that would be potentially challenging or even embarrassing for them not to know about.
- Ask for their help and guidance when you're getting stuck or need a second opinion.
- Notify them when things go wrong or when you or your team have made a serious mistake.
- Let them know what you've been working on and make sure that your priorities are aligned so that you can course-correct as necessary.
- Let them know about your teams and where team members are excelling or struggling.
- Enlist their support in developing opportunities for your team.
- Ask to be included on projects or initiatives that provide you with growth and development opportunities.
- Ask them how you're doing and how you could enhance your performance or be more helpful to them.

Organizational structure, achieving role clarity, and determining the right levels of management and hierarchy

Working in a hybrid or remote environment could prompt changes to your organizational structure. You may determine that changed business needs support a move to more regional or global roles and that you need to restructure and retrain your team accordingly. Or, you may need more team members with remote training or other capabilities that enable your team to maintain or increase their impact in the absence of in-person time.

Take this opportunity to revisit your organizational structure, including reporting relationships, titles, and job descriptions. Take a first pass at this exercise while focusing exclusively on your needs, without envisioning specific team members in specific roles. This is called a blank-sheet approach and it helps you to envision transformative change, rather than iterative or incremental adjustments. Then, once you've charted out the ideal future organization, adjust it to fit your team and capabilities. In this way, you can balance your current reality with a longer-term directional move to your ideal organizational structure.

Start with or pay special attention to building your leadership team. Do you have the right capabilities now across the team and, if not, do you have rising stars who you could develop? Think about your research needs as well as technical or operations' needs, including emerging areas that you may need to add newer skills to cover, like data analytics or application program interfaces (APIs). Consider succession planning for your team as well and think about the future leaders who may be ready to move into different roles in one, three, or five years. Involving junior team members in projects helps you to identify future leaders, but you should also have conversations with them to determine where they would like their careers to go. Success on discrete projects isn't always an indicator of leadership acumen or of desire to be a manager, so ensure that you're having honest and realistic discussions with your team members about their career goals.

You should also pay attention to the sub-functions within your current structure. Does your team provide research exclusively for the firm's clients and legal matters, or does it also provide competitive intelligence or market research to help identify new business opportunities? If you have research teams with differing remits, can you use this opportunity to cross-train and enable them to work more closely together? Having more team members with a broader range of research experience can help you to be nimbler in responding to internal and external client needs. Structural or organizational change could help you to combine your teams under a broader structure and with an expanded scope. Added benefits include development opportunities for team members as well as more varied and interesting work.

You should also consider whether you can tailor in-office requirements to specific roles and lessen or eliminate the requirement to be in the office for other roles, allowing you to recruit more effectively and bring on higher levels of talent by offering increased flexibility.

Once you have thought through your needs and ideal organizational structure, you'll need to assure that you have the necessary degree of buy-in and support from your firm's leadership. You'll also need to have a realistic plan for managing the degree of change required. Transitioning to a hybrid environment provides more opportunities to de-silo and to work cross-culturally and across time zones, but it takes time and patience to foster the collaboration, teamwork, and alignment you will need in order to be successful.

You will likely find that you need to be flexible and periodically adjust your plan, because remote working is not right for everyone and will not be successful across the board. Recognizing when hybrid or remote working is not appropriate for a specific role or team member and making necessary schedule changes while also considering other factors like parity across the team is challenging, and working with your HR team to adjust as necessary is recommended.

Tips for fostering a cross-cultural team environment

How do you provide the level of internal communication needed to maintain a healthy and engaged team in a remote or hybrid working environment? Similarly, how do you ensure that your function remains top-of-mind to users of your services instead of "out of sight, out of mind?"

Communicating frequently and in different ways across your global team should be a priority. Here are a few tips for you to consider:

- Use all-hands calls with a wide range of speakers and viewpoints to build engagement and collaboration and include some topics that are "just for fun".
- Ensure that your team's skills are being refreshed consistently with a variety of training opportunities, ranging from soft-skills training to vendor training or professional association conferences.
- Send frequent team emails and updates and keep in mind that they do not always have to be focused on work. Photos of vacations, families, hobbies etc. can build collegiality and connection across a physically scattered team.
- Achieve the right amount of "face time" in a remote or hybrid environment by continuing to plan meaningful office visits. Although it's unlikely that we'll ever match our pre-COVID travel schedules, it's hard to match face-to-face interactions for building lasting connections.
- Increase the number of lawyer-facing communications, training on new research tools, research team support, and key offerings. Use a variety of approaches, including in-person, recording, Zoom, and one-on-one screen-sharing sessions.
- Increasingly, our external clients are expressing interest in our wide range of research tools and expert researchers, and they frequently ask about them in pitches and requests for proposals (RFPs). They are

also interested in horizon-scanning offerings, for example, legislative or regulatory monitoring. Many in-house lawyers miss the research tools and support that they had when they were in firms, and they would welcome the opportunity to have a level of access to them. (Note that you will need to ensure that you have the appropriate licensing in place before sharing access to research databases and products with clients.) These client-facing research offerings can be provided as value-adds or in some cases they can be revenue-generating. Not only will these service offerings please clients and help to forge stronger client relationships, but they will also help your team develop new skills and increase your team's visibility and value within the firm.

Practical and operational considerations to facilitate remote working

Listed below are a few operational changes to consider that will help you manage your remote team more successfully.

- First, if you don't already have a workflow management tool or ticketing system in place that enables you to manage and report on incoming requests, working remotely across offices and time zones will necessitate adoption of a tool to do this. The benefits include:
  - The ability to triage work appropriately across the globe based on expertise, bandwidth, or other factors;
  - The ability to cross-train and pair experienced researchers with more junior team members on specific requests; and
  - The ability to report on your team's work, including to track productivity and trends and manage to your team's KPIs.
- Most law libraries have already realized many of the benefits of moving away from print access to digital, a development hastened by the move to remote working. In line with the move towards digital access to research tools, the need to ensure that your firm has the right complement of research tools and that they are licensed appropriately has become a higher priority. Wherever financially practical, obtaining global licensing provides the most flexibility and value for a firm with many offices across the globe.
- Offshoring, outsourcing, and using consultants is a more realistic and effective option in a hybrid or remote environment. As mentioned above, being free of requirements to be in the office full-time offers the

potential to retain outsourced researchers or consultants to handle overflow, after-hours, or weekend research requests, providing extra bandwidth as needed.

What new opportunities can your team realize in this changed environment?

Although managing a remote research team is not without challenges, the benefits of working in this environment outweigh the disadvantages in many cases. Some strong benefits include the following:

- You may now have the ability to recruit from anywhere, or at least from anywhere within a reasonable distance to an existing office.
- You can support your team in having more balanced lives, including enabling them to manage childcare or other personal needs more easily, or to work in a time zone that is most aligned with their personal preference.
- You have an opportunity to reevaluate your team's research offerings and tools and potentially to enhance them or to standardize them more broadly across offices and regions.
- You can have a broader global impact by providing regional or global training.
- You can offer new client-facing and revenue-generating research services.
- You can view your team's skills and capabilities broadly and develop team members for the roles of tomorrow, such as data analytics and managing APIs to build new research products.

As fraught and chaotic as the abrupt move to remote work was, it has created lasting change and in some of the areas mentioned above we can build on these changes to derive transformational benefits, including developing and providing opportunities to our teams and helping to build more compelling and visible offerings to our internal and external clients.

Chapter 15:
Law firm knowledge management and the metaverse

By Anthony J. Rhem, CEO and principal consultant, AJ Rhem & Associates Inc.

Introduction

The metaverse is becoming integrated into the consciousness of businesses and will become prominent for the future of work. It is a virtual space where people can work, play, shop, and socialize, just like we do in the real-world (or real-life). It promises to be another world where we all can do things such as travel, go to concerts, take training classes, or converse with colleagues, feeling like you're really there, and feeling like other people are really there with you. This virtual environment also promises to create a new working environment in the same way. As this new future evolves, so will law firm management, particularly the delivery of knowledge. Law firm knowledge management is driven by collaboration and using knowledge effectively. The metaverse will increase the geographic reach of lawyers and law firms, enabling an increased access to knowledge.

Law firms in the metaverse

Businesses, relationships, property ownership, and other situations that are handled legally in the real world are similarly handled legally in the metaverse. Law firms must be familiar with how it works since, as clients thrive and do their business in this space, there will be a need for lawyers and law firms to provide services and set up offices there. Some examples of legal work that could be done in the metaverse include real estate closings, marriage certificates, divorces, property disputes, and trademark conflicts, to name a few. If a law firm chooses not to operate in this environment, an understanding of how it works and what legal services are being done will still be beneficial in addressing these clients' needs.[1]

The metaverse also has legal implications. A few noteworthy concerns include fraudulent transactions, compromised data, invasion of privacy, and unregulated spaces, as well as other legal and ethical issues not yet known.[2] This is the case with any new technology, especially one that is creating a whole new, albeit virtual, world. We could also see many legal applications that automate client intake combined with specific legal knowledge to create automated solutions that will assist lawyers in delivering legal advice. The metaverse and the ability of cloud-based platforms to automate and implement technology will enable a more sophisticated level of work, merging technology with automated processes and legal knowledge that will prove beneficial for lawyers working in this space.

While there is much research to be done in this area, there is an opportunity for legal practitioners to be part of shaping the evolving landscape that could benefit how lawyers and law firms interact with and retain clients in this environment. The metaverse is set to expand as more users and businesses enter it, which will lead to an increase in legal and regulatory issues. Consequently, law firms that already have a strong foundation will prove invaluable to clients.[3]

KM in the metaverse

Knowledge management (KM) is designed to enable people and organizations to collaborate, share, create, and use knowledge, and leveraged to improve performance, increase innovation, and grow the knowledge base of both people and the organization.[4] In the metaverse, knowledge management will take hold and be adopted across the law firm in an immersive environment with the possibility of accelerating knowledge management's effectiveness. Technology will play an important role in the success of law firms in the metaverse; having a stable virtual environment with access to the technology tools that lawyers need to execute their jobs effectively will be essential. This chapter examines how law firm knowledge management will be affected by the metaverse.

Metaverse drivers for law firm knowledge management

Advances in law technology have revolutionized today's legal landscape, as has the evolution of the legal professional. Developments in legal services technology have impacted every aspect of the legal field, from law firm and corporate practice to the courtroom. As the metaverse becomes more widely adopted within law firms as well as by legal practitioners, and as the practice of law becomes disrupted through the use of and advances in the metaverse, we must consider what will drive law firms and legal practitioners to this environment.

The following details what is driving law firms to consider the metaverse, and the possible role of KM:

- *Cost pressures.* KM can be used to work more efficiently to meet client demands and become more cost effective.
- *Efficiency and consistency.* KM through collaboration and knowledge capture will become more efficient in delivering services to more potential clients.
- *Flexibility and responsiveness.* KM will facilitate flexibility and responsiveness to client needs by assigning the "right resources" (lawyers) at the right time in the right way to address the particular need(s) of clients.
- *Training and learning.* KM, in particular knowledge transfer, knowledge sharing, and collaboration processes, policies, and tools will create an atmosphere where lawyers can learn from each other, share best practices, and provide practical training in a simulated and immersive environment.
- *Retention (people and knowledge).* Successful KM practices, policies, and tools will create an environment where all staff will experience enrichment through collaboration and sharing. In addition, expertise management can be improved. Lawyers will be assigned to cases where their expertise can be best leveraged, which will foster an environment where the retention of staff is high. Individual knowledge will be captured and included as part of the corporate knowledge base where it can be accessed across the firm, and this will facilitate the retention of the firm's knowledge.
- *Workplace satisfaction.* There is the potential for an increase in the accessibility of knowledge, which contributes greatly towards workplace satisfaction. The metaverse will foster an environment where sharing knowledge and open communication for collaboration will continue to enrich the workplace.

Legal research in the metaverse

Lawyers must have access to fully integrated products and services, enabling smarter, faster decisions and confident action for clients and organizations. This access must support the firm's legal research process. According to the CALI Law Books Sources of American Law, the legal research process consists of five basic steps. These five basic research steps can be applied to almost any research initiative. They provide structure for legal research and apply to conducting legal research in the metaverse, which at a minimum must support these steps to enable lawyers to execute research.

The five steps consist of:

1. *Familiarize yourself with the specifics of the legal problem.*
2. *Define the scope of the research.*
3. *Construct search queries.*
4. *Gather primary authorities.*
5. *Analyze and update primary authorities.*[5]

As you begin to understand where to find the right content, which is buried deep within your firm's thousands of research repositories and outside sources, and who in the firm has deep knowledge of specific content, in addition to wondering if what you have in your repositories is up-to-date and relevant, you quickly realize that knowledge management is a challenge! Multiply that by the number of trial and appellate briefs, memoranda, pleadings, depositions, emails, letters, and spreadsheets prepared by inside and outside counsel alike and the challenge becomes even more daunting. Having access to these research elements inside the metaverse is the new challenge. Everything must be accessible electronically. Without incorporating KM in driving your metaverse access to digital assets, your firm runs the risk of paying for research over and over again.

Legal research tools

During the early years of a lawyer's career, research and document drafting are the predominant professional activities performed. Legal research tools and sources are key to assisting early stage lawyers in performing their tasks. The tools of legal research are considered knowledge management tools that help legal professionals locate the knowledge and analysis previously written by judges, expert scholars, and lawyers for adaptation and use in the context presented by a current client. Legal research platforms, which include citation tools, treatises by authors and competitive publishers, as well as integrated search functionality, must all be delivered in the metaverse to legal researchers.

The benefits of legal research tools include being able to deliver an increase in research speed and accuracy as well as enabling a precision of collaboration that the combination of research resources and tools makes possible. Realizing the benefits that the various legal research tools bring to the law firm will depend in large measure on how the metaverse for the law firm and legal practitioner is structured. It can contain a multitude of various capabilities and spaces, providing its inhabitants with access to what they need. Therefore it is important that the metaverse environment that is built (structured) for lawyers has the necessary access to tools to support the practice of law. Access to the firm's internal data and its systems will be essential for the success of any law firm operating in this immersive environment.

Having access to judicial precedent/case law information and incorporating that knowledge within the overall knowledge management infrastructure is crucial for law firm performance. Again, the ability to provide this in the metaverse is another important research tool for law firms and legal practitioners.

Law firm collaboration in the metaverse

The metaverse offers law firms and legal practitioners an immersive form of interaction and collaboration with seamless interactions between people all over the world. In the metaverse, legal staff and clients can present themselves however they feel confident and comfortable, which is empowering and provides the opportunity for free exchange of information, knowledge, and ideas. These interactions can also be more authentic and trust-building than face-to-face conversations, often stifled by social anxieties and issues with authority. The law firm business models that are most likely to succeed from a collaborative perspective are those firms that already have strong collaboration culture. However, with the right focus and intent, including the right tools and technologies, the possibilities for effective collaboration in the metaverse are much higher.[6]

Many lawyers will have an opportunity to gain exposure to the metaverse using Mesh for Microsoft Teams®, an enhancement that adds virtual reality/metaverse features to Microsoft's Teams product. Microsoft indicates that the combination of Teams and virtual reality technologies will produce better collaboration, more participant engagement, and an improved three-dimensional interface.[7] Mesh-enabled Teams users will also be able to manipulate virtual objects during conference sessions, and engage with eye contact, facial expressions, and gestures when using VR headsets and motion capture devices.

One prevalent issue with remote communication currently is the loss of non-verbal cues and interpretations gained from reading body language, which inhibit our understanding of each other. In the metaverse, all that will change. We'll be able to create highly realistic 3D avatars that will be virtual representations of ourselves and mirror our body language. This will facilitate remote meetings that feel as though you and your colleagues really are sharing the same room, enhancing communication, trust and authentic connection. Additionally, this can bring senior leaders and associates together to form the kinds of connections that don't usually happen via a screen. The ability to share a virtual space, and a wide range of virtual objects, also unlocks huge benefits when it comes to law firm collaboration and the sharing of information, knowledge, and insights.[8]

The metaverse allows a new, and radical, democracy of space and physical presence, which can have a profound effect on the law firm organization's culture. Law firms and legal practitioners will have shared "metaversal" spaces, and the opportunities they offer to bring people together in new ways will affect the law firm culture and the way work is done.[9]

Legal and ethical issues of law firm KM in the metaverse

So, what are the legal issues the metaverse will bring in the future? At this time, we can only guess what legal questions will arise as we interact in this new environment, including in relation to the technology and possible applications of the metaverse itself. The following are some of the legal issues we need to consider:

- *Data protection law.* New types of data will be processed, such as facial expressions, gestures, and other physiological reactions to certain content and events within the metaverse. How will this data be protected and secured?
- *Competition law.* How can companies advertise their products?
- *Copyright law.* What must be observed when digital assets are embodied as non-fungible tokens (NFT), or real buildings replicated in the metaverse?
- *Securities and banking supervisory law.* This concerns licensing and prospectus obligations for trading digital assets.
- *Tax law.* This concerns income from renting virtual land.
- *General civil and criminal law.* Will it be treated the same as in the real world?[10]

The metaverse and knowledge continuity in law firms

"Analogous to business continuity, which refers to ensuring that operations are backed up should a catastrophic event render the business no longer operational (e.g. a fire), Knowledge continuity refers to ensuring that no critical

> *knowledge is lost due to employees leaving the firm (due to a retirement, resignation, or other reason).*"[11]

Knowledge continuity is an important part of any law firm's practice of delivering legal services to its clients. Mechanisms to provide for knowledge continuity in the metaverse should adopt the law firm's current knowledge continuity strategy, along with the processes and tools that are being used.

The value of preserving institutional knowledge should not be underestimated. Putting in place a system that retains business and operational knowledge prevents having to reinvent the wheel for knowledge procedures and policies when an outside force causes chaos. Technology exists to continually capture, curate, and store institutional knowledge and make it readily accessible to the people who need it. In the metaverse, to ensure knowledge continuity, access to these systems is imperative.

Conclusion and key points to consider

As mentioned in the introduction to this chapter, as the future of the metaverse evolves, so will law firm management, particularly the delivery of knowledge. The metaverse no doubt will be the catalyst for lawyers and law firms to collaborate and reach beyond their current geographic boundaries. It will evolve as more users and business enter and incorporate it into their real world. This evolution will come with legal and regulatory issues, and users and businesses in the metaverse will greatly benefit from law firms that have already incorporated it into their practice. The following are some key points to consider:

- Before beginning the journey, consider what legal questions will arise as we interact in this new environment, including the technology and possible applications of the metaverse itself.
- When considering incorporating the metaverse in the law firm/law practice, begin with the benefits and pitfalls it can bring. Identify the key benefits and align them to the metaverse drivers to guide the decision-making process.
- The way law firms operate and the way legal professionals work will be transformed. Acquiring the right technology professionals to assist in developing the metaverse and transitioning technology into this virtual environment, as well as providing the necessary training to all legal staff, will facilitate adoption and proper use and interaction. Law firms must partner with experienced technology firms that deliver metaverse technology and development.

- Training programs must be established to assist all law firm management team members to understand the new environment and to work in a more technologically advanced and collaborative way.
- A best practice for instituting any technology is to start with a pilot with a few lawyers in order to demonstrate its value for your firm.
- Understanding your law firm's culture as well as the people in your firm's ability to adopt new technology and new ways of working will be the key to success in the metaverse.

References

1 National Law Review (2022). Law Firms and the Metaverse: Should you buy property? www.natlawreview.com/article/law-firms-and-metaverse-should-you-buy-property

2 *Ibid.*

3 *Ibid.*

4 Rhem, A.J. AI ethics and its impact on knowledge management. *AI Ethics* 1, 33-37 (2021). https://doi.org/10.1007/s43681-020-00015-2

5 The Center for Computer Assisted Legal Instruction (CALI). (nd). CALI Lawbooks Sources of American Law. https://sourcesofamericanlaw.lawbooks.cali.org/chapter/the-research-process/

6 Mike Prokopeak, "How the Metaverse Will Usher in a New Era of Collaboration", www.reworked.co/collaboration-productivity/how-the-metaverse-will-usher-in-a-new-era-of-collaboration/amp/.

7 Roach, J. (2021). Mesh for Microsoft Teams aims to make collaboration in the "metaverse" personal and fun. https://news.microsoft.com/innovation-stories/mesh-for-microsoft-teams/

8 Workplace, "How we'll work in the metaverse", https://en-gb.workplace.com/blog/how-we-work-in-the-metaverse.

9 *Ibid.*

10 CMS Law-Now™ (2022). Legal advice in the metaverse. www.cms-lawnow.com/ealerts/2022/01/legal-advice-in-the-metaverse

11 Rhem, A. J. (2016). *Knowledge Management in Practice*. CRC Press; www.igi-global.com/dictionary/the-role-of-human-resources-hr-in-tacit-knowledge-sharing/59218.

About Globe Law and Business

Globe Law and Business was established in 2005. From the very beginning, we set out to create law books that are sufficiently high level to be of real use to the experienced professional, yet still accessible and easy to navigate. Most of our authors are drawn from Magic Circle and other top commercial firms, both in the United Kingdom and internationally.

Our titles are carefully produced, with the utmost attention paid to editorial, design and production processes. We hope this results in high-quality publications that are easy to read and a pleasure to own. Our titles are also available as ebooks, which are compatible with most desktop, laptop and tablet devices. In 2018 we expanded our portfolio to include journals and Special Reports, available both digitally and in hard copy format, and produced to the same high standards as our books.

In 2021, we were very pleased to announce the start of a new chapter for Globe Law and Business following the acquisition of law books under the imprint Ark Publishing. Our law firm management list is now significantly expanded with many well known and loved Ark Publishing titles.

We are also pleased to announce the launch of our online content platform, Globe Law Online. This allows for easy search and networked access across firms. Key collections include the Law Firm Management Collection, Private Client and Energy and the Energy Transition. Email me at sian@globelawandbusiness.com for further details or to arrange a free trial for you or your firm.

Sian O'Neill
Managing director
Globe Law and Business
www.globelawandbusiness.com

Related titles

Globe Law and Business

Go to **www.globelawandbusiness.com**
for full details including free sample chapters